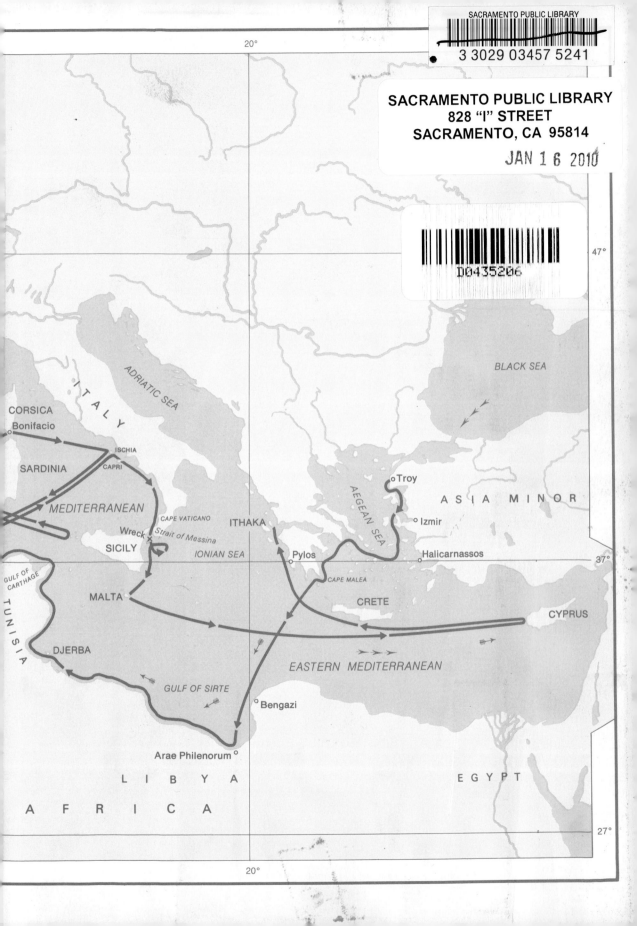

20°

47°

BLACK SEA

ADRIATIC SEA

ITALY

CORSICA
Bonifacio

ISCHIA

SARDINIA
CAPRI

MEDITERRANEAN

CAPE VATICANO
ITHAKA

Troy

AEGEAN SEA

ASIA MINOR

Izmir

Wreck
Strait of Messina
SICILY
IONIAN SEA
Pylos
Halicarnassos
37°

GULF OF
CARTHAGE
CAPE MALEA
CRETE
CYPRUS

TUNISIA
MALTA

DJERBA
EASTERN MEDITERRANEAN

GULF OF SIRTE

Bengazi

Arae Philenorum

LIBYA
EGYPT

AFRICA

27°

20°

ULYSSES AIRBORNE

ULYSSES AIRBORNE

MAURICIO OBREGÓN

With an Introduction by Samuel Eliot Morison
Photographs by Cristina Martínez-Irujo de Obregón

HARPER & ROW, PUBLISHERS
New York, Evanston, San Francisco, London

The photograph on page 171 is published by permission of the Director of Antiquities and the Cyprus Museum. The photograph on page 173 is published courtesy of James F. Nields of N.A.A. and Vincent J. Oliver of N.E.S.C.

Seventeen quotations from *The Odyssey* translated by E. V. Rieu appear as extracts in type smaller than that of the text and are reprinted by permission of Penguin Books Ltd. Copyright E. V. Rieu, 1946.

Maps by Jean Paul Tremblay

FIRST EDITION

STANDARD BOOK NUMBER: 06-013232-9

LIBRARY OF CONGRESS CATALOG CARD NUMBER: 71-156541

Designed by Patricia Dunbar

To Navsikaa,
who loves but lets live

CONTENTS

PHOTOGRAPHS

CHARTS

Ulysses, my lord, spare me your praise of Death. If I could only return to earth, I would rather be the serf of some landless man, who himself has little enough to live on, than king of all these dead men whose lives are done.

—Achilles to Ulysses, *The Odyssey*, Book XI

INTRODUCTION

This book is a happy welding of technique to scholarship. It is the work of a humane and intelligent scholar, steeped in the culture of both worlds, who is also a highly competent Colombian sailor, meteorologist, and an aviator high up in his profession. *Ulysses Airborne* means just what it says: a series of flights around and across the Mediterranean to identify and photograph the places where Ulysses touched in his several ships and rafts. It opens with a stimulating and scholarly description of the Homeric world—ships, houses, furniture, wine and food, marriage customs, law, and religion—the best that I have had the good fortune to read during the seventy-odd years that I have been a Homer aficionado. For I began reading *The Odyssey* long before Linear-A, Linear-B, and the tablets had been discovered, or before archaeology had developed new techniques, or skindivers had begun working over Homeric wrecks. Obregón has assimilated all this new literature, which in many respects has explained details in *The Odyssey* hitherto obscure or much disputed. For instance, he points out that the description of the ship built by Ulysses at Ogygia (V. 235–63) agrees with that of a recently explored Mycenaean wreck off Cape Gelydonia, even to the bulwarks of willow withes which so puzzled the scholiasts. We now know far more about the Homeric world than did the scholars of the nineteenth century.

Chapter II, in which we start home with Ulysses, begins with a discussion of his initial course across the Aegean. One of Obregón's most valuable instruments is his knowledge, both from sailing and flying, of Mediterranean winds. Thus he does not make the mistake of earlier Homeric commentators, making Ulysses' ship sail in any direction to suit the author, as if she had an auxiliary engine and not a mere bank of oars to help the sail.

We are continually whisked back from the Homeric age to the Obregóns today, and one of their most amusing experiences was their exploration by air and minijeep of Mallorca. Mauricio leaves no doubt in the reader's mind that this major island of the Balearics was the home of Polyphemos the Cyclops. For Homer's teasing phrase about an island where "the outgoings of the night and of the day are close together" (X. 86), which has led some overenthusiastic commentators to take Ulysses to the Land of the Midnight Sun, Obregón has a common-sense explanation: a shepherd leading his flock out of its daytime folds in a Mallorcan cave might encounter another bringing home the cattle from daytime pasture to spend the night in the same natural barn.

In his Chapter IV the author tells once more the charming story of Ulysses meeting white-armed Navsikaa, and he places the double port of her father's island kingdom in Cyprus, birthplace of Aphrodite. He also convinces us that Ulysses' Ithaka was indeed the modern Ithaka, and can even identify the landing place when he finally reached home and was recognized only by the swineherd and his old dog.

Chapter V is of particular interest to sailors, amateur or professional, for therein Obregón applies nautical astronomy to Ulysses' problems of navigation. The wily one remembered how high the navigators' favorite stars—Arcturus, Vega, Capella, and the rest—circled over Ithaka, so that by observing their altitudes at various points of his long voyage he could tell, roughly, whether he was north or south of the latitude of his home port, and shape his course accordingly (V. 270–76). Thus the Northmen navigated from Norway to Greenland and North America, like Ulysses, without benefit of compass. Our author explains all this in language that anyone can understand, and accompanies it by a celestial chart; to check it, he had the heavens switched back to 700 B.C. and earlier, especially for him, by the Hayden Planetarium in New York, and his conclusions may well put an end to more than two thousand years of argument about Homer and where he wrote his poems.

The whole book is full of intimate and charming touches about the

Obregóns' personal experiences during their Odyssey. Mauricio and Lita have such a feeling for the beauty of Homer's narrative and the Homeric country that one feels even the jealous gods would approve, and shield them from disaster on future flights.

In conclusion, this book introduces a new, scientifically minded generation to one of the greatest poems of all time, and provides lovers of Homer with scientific confirmation that the blind bard spoke the truth.

SAMUEL ELIOT MORISON

PROLOGUE

Only a woman could love the wily Ulysses, a woman or a goddess—a distinction sometimes difficult for us mortals, but not for Homer, who so carefully portrayed Penelope the woman, Navsikaa the girl, Circe the sorceress, and Kalypso the nymph. Yet all of them pitied and loved Ulysses; for in those hardheaded times, passion and compassion had not yet been separated by fear of sentimental softness, a fear unnatural to a race of semifeudal warriors who wept openly at public banquets. If anyone was in danger of becoming soft in those days, it was the gods.

A man, on the other hand, may admire or even envy Ulysses, but in the end his reaction will be that of the hunter. Once confronted with this man-sized god who stands, tangible in his reality, at the very origin of that cumulative self-portrait we call literature, a man must feel a mounting need to follow and to capture him, even if only because, like Everest, "he is there." And there he is, and real. Real as the poet who picked him out of the memories of his people, to thrust upon him the eternity that Ulysses refused to accept even from fair Kalypso.

But of his origin so little is known that many have disputed this reality, relegating both the poet and his hero to the twilight of myth or to the limbo of a plural tradition without identity; and as to the setting and origin of *The Odyssey*, the argument between rival islands and cities has no end. Yet of the unity and reality of *The Odyssey* and therefore of its author there are, to me, many indications, not the least of which lies in the way the poem is constructed, for Homer begins by asking the Muse to tell the story in whatever order she pleases, and then proceeds to unfold his poem in the most dramatic and least obvious way.

In chapters I through IV [1] he tells of the coming of age of Telemachos,

1. The division of Homer into chapters or "books" is Alexandrian.

Ulysses' son, who last saw his father when he sailed for Troy, almost twenty years before. The place is now full of Penelope's impertinent suitors, and though the clever queen has managed to hold them at bay with her famous web, no one has challenged them until her son dares to convene a popular assembly, and then sails off in search of news of his father. All this he does under the prodding and protection of Athena, Ulysses' own defender before her father Zeus. First they visit old King Nestor at sandy Pylos, and then they join red-haired King Menelaos and his still-fair Helen at the wedding feast of their children in the splendid palace at Sparta. This part of the poem serves principally to set the scene by describing the Mycenaean world, and to capture the reader's interest through skillful "flashbacks" to the Trojan war and tempting foretastes of the adventures to come. And at its end we are carefully left in suspense as to whether the suitors' deathtrap for Telemachos will be successful or not.

Next, in chapters V through XIII, the poem turns to homesick Ulysses, about to be rescued by Hermes from the distant island of Ogygia, at the very center of the world, where he has spent seven years with Kalypso, some willing and some not; and then proceeds to describe the rest of his adventures until his arrival in Ithaka. This is the body of our "sailing directions," largely presented by Ulysses himself at the marvelous court of King Alkinoös, father of Navsikaa; and it is mainly on the information contained in this part of the poem, as well as on much to be found in other parts, that I have based my search for Ulysses' itinerary.

Finally, in chapters XIV through XXIV, the poet watches Ulysses' homecoming, releases us from our doubts concerning the fate of his son, and works up to their bloody revenge upon the suitors, a dramatic climax comparable to the great duel that crowns every proper Western.

To me, this method of developing the story clearly shows an overall plan of the highest dramatic and poetic qualities, and I am led to conclude that Homer's poem was composed in a single act of artistic creation, or at least, if the elements of the story had been handed down for generations in several bardic songs as seems probable, that a single poet did in fact put them all together in the most artful form, conserving the many "ready-made" phrases that made it possible to recite or sing the entire poem from memory.

So much for the unity of the poem itself. But the reality of Homer's world has more recently increased beyond doubt with every stone turned at Troy by Schliemann, that most gifted of amateurs, who in our century confirmed the basic truth of Homer's geography, and, some twenty years ago, with every word deciphered by another nonprofessional, Michael Ventris, whose discovery of the language of thousands of tablets found at Knossos, Mykene, and Pylos (and later elsewhere) has brought further confirmation of the details of Homer's story. So, doubt as to whether Ulysses or Homer ever existed I will leave to others. And anyhow, who can stalk a tiger without a growing sense that the beast is real?

Yet to most people Homer's story is still no more than a charming poem of adventure, whose mysterious though detailed itinerary has been pursued in vain by all manner of passionate scholars and studious amateurs, on foot, on horseback, and under sail, ever since the ancients produced that marvelous blending of history and poetry we have so nearly lost. So my aim here is modest only in its simplicity: to use the modern magic of flight and today's knowledge of navigation, astronomy, meteorology, ancient history, archaeology, and linguistics to propose a cogent itinerary for the Odyssey and a home port for its author.

And why should I dare to challenge this ancient riddle in, of all things, an airplane? It all started with Columbus. Eight years ago Samuel Eliot Morison and his charming wife Priscilla came to Colombia, and we went sailing together out of Cartagena de Indias with Hernán Echavarría and my cousin Rafael Obregón, twice South American sailing champion. I had flown down from Bogotá to meet them in my airplane, a five-place Cessna 310 whose identification, "HK 960 P," had been reduced to the nickname *Oh Papa*, from the old phonetic pronunciation of its last two figures.

In this company of sailors, the conversation soon turned from navigation to aviation and to history when Sam and I talked of flying out low over the Caribbean in *Oh Papa*, to check the visibility of the Sierra Nevada de Santa Marta from the eye level of a ship's lookout. The Sierra raises its eternal snows to an altitude of nineteen thousand feet, eleven degrees north of the equator, practically on the same longitude as the islands of San Salvador and Hispaniola, and only twenty-five miles from Colombia's Caribbean shore—all of which had made me wonder why it did not figure earlier in the history of the discovery. Thus began *Oh Papa*'s small contribution to the field of experimental history, to which Morison has contributed so much; for during our flight back it occurred to us that, if in a couple of hours we had been able to photograph one landmark exactly as it might have looked from a ship, there was no reason why we should not similarly document all the places mentioned by Columbus and by his men, using our aerial mobility to confirm or correct their identifications, many of which had been proposed by Morison himself during the Harvard-Columbus expedition of 1939.

Twenty thousand air miles later, three hundred photographs by David Crofoot and by Lita, my wife, did the job in our book *The Caribbean as Columbus Saw It*.[2] At least one new identification we made from *Oh Papa* is already widely accepted: Cabo Tiburón in Colombia for Columbus's last night on the continent, which adds a whole coast and one modern nation (mine) to his discoveries. Since then we have studied from Jim Nields' airplane the various voyages to North America Morison describes in *The European Discovery of America: The Northern Voyages*, and are now working on the southern discoverers and Magellan. But since I have always felt that God only made two seas to the scale of man for his enjoyment, making the others mere lakes or boundless oceans, my memories of days spent flying around the Caribbean in

2. Atlantic–Little, Brown, 1964.

The New *Oh Papa*, Photographer, and Author

search of Columbus soon brought Lita, myself, and a new *Oh Papa* to my other favorite, the Mediterranean, in search of the other great mariner, Ulysses, with Sam and Priscilla Morison as godparents of our project.

This book, then, is an invitation to fly with us in search of the routes of *The Odyssey*. This "divertimento" will put us in contact once more with the beautiful world from which our civilization sprang, and that in itself would be worthwhile since our everyday sense of beauty is full of atavistic memories of that world, however deadened they may be by our noisy century. And our contemplation will be spiced by our role as airborne detectives, a job not far removed from the historian's (the Greek root of the word *history* means "to inquire"). Further, our aircraft will give us mobility comparable only with that of the messenger Hermes, while most of those who went before us were limited to the speed of windblown canvas or of galloping horse—speeds, it is interesting to note, never exceeded by man until close to the dawn of this century.

This extraordinary mobility will enable us to avoid the common trap of fitting facts to theory, for we will observe Ulysses' world from all necessary angles, climbing high for a "map" or skimming the waves for a sailor's view. And every time we find one of our identifications unsatisfactory we will simply keep flying until we find a better one, modifying our theory accordingly; something that none of our predecessors could do unless he wished to spend a whole lifetime afloat. We will cover fifty thousand miles in a few summers, and another modern tool will document our findings in a way that is at the same time new and immemorial: Lita's photographs[3] will give us a lasting picture of Ulysses' ports of call almost as he might have remembered them, for surely the language of images still came to his uncluttered mind as naturally as that of words, which certainly never failed him. (We ourselves are only now returning to this image-language, after many generations of words,

3. The earliest existing aerial photograph was taken about 1860 by James Wallace Black, from a balloon two thousand feet above Boston.

thanks to the rapid spread of pictorial communications.) Thus will we try to preserve the sense of momentary reincarnation that all art, great or small, must try to produce.

I will not now mention the names of all who have gone before us in this quest, for they are too many and too well known, but I do pause to acknowledge my debt to all of them, while referring the reader to the short bibliography with which this book closes. Here I will simply mention some of the friends who have given special support to this project:

Among the scholars without whose encouragement I might not have dared to proceed, I have already mentioned Samuel Eliot Morison, from whom I learned to avoid theorizing about historical places without first having a good look at them. Next must come Professor Spyridon Marinatos, Director of Antiquities of Greece, and Dr. Emily Vermeule, then of the Boston Museum of Fine Arts and now at Harvard, who introduced me to him; V. Karageorghis, Marinatos' counterpart in Cyprus; Francisco Martí of the Archaeological Museum of Barcelona; the late María Luisa Serra, Director of Archaeology of Minorca; Professor William Diver of the Linguistics Department of Columbia University; N. Klissiotis, chief of the Meteorological Service of Athens; and Kenneth L. Franklin, assistant director of the Hayden Planetarium in New York. All were indispensable, but I must make it clear that none can be held responsible for my conclusions.

In Bogotá, Nicolás Gomez, Enrique Uribe White, Professor Rafi Lation, Rafael Obregón, and Alec Bright; in New York, Malcolm Wiener, Frances Lindley, and Flora Klein; in Ware, Massachusetts, Jim Nields; in Paris, Victor Najar and Carlos Aristimuño; in St. Moritz and St. Tropez (where I was shipwrecked), the late Fritz von Opel; and in Gstaad, Leonard Woods; all gave enthusiastically of their knowledge and advice.

As to my fellow airmen, Ian Forbes, president of Piper International in Geneva, made it possible for me to rent two successive Piper Turbo-Twin Comanches to substitute for the original *Oh Papa*; Maurice and

Monique Baird-Smith flew with me around the Aegean, Turkey, and Cyprus in their own Cessna Skylane; and four airlines, Avianca, Pan Am, Swissair, and Iberia greatly facilitated my long-range travel. It was largely on their sumptuous jets that I checked the first drafts of this text, and the excellence of their wines may serve to excuse its defects, which I hope will not scare away too many scholars.

To E. V. Rieu I owe a special debt for my use of seventeen passages from his beautiful modern translation of *The Odyssey*. The remaining translations are my own, and I must also take full responsibility for my comfortably arbitrary "phonetic" spelling of Greek names, which attempts to render modern conclusions as to how the ancient Greeks pronounced their wonderful language. This knowledge had been lost until the new linguists began to string the necklace of succeeding languages and to note the way each spelled words from its immediate predecessor, in order to connect unknown pronunciation to known. I shall be sorry if readers more accustomed to a traditional orthography react as do some admirers of the sober Parthenon when they find out that in its day it glowed in polychrome.

It is impossible to list all those whose hospitality constantly reminded Lita and myself that wanderers are favorites of Zeus; but I hope that all who have borne patiently with my endless talk of past, present, and future will enjoy this "final" report on a quest that I am sure will never end. For if I am willing to propose a new itinerary for Ulysses and a new base for Homer, I am nevertheless happy to admit that in this field there may never be a last word. Which is one of the reasons why Ulysses will never die.

So to the chase. But first, in Chapter I, a brief description of Ulysses' world and a summary of the story of its rediscovery. In succeeding chapters I will take Ulysses' voyage in chronological order (not in Homer's) and propose identifications to fit the surprisingly complete descriptions contained in *The Odyssey*, which I will confront with real coasts, ports, winds, currents, and navigational stars. I will explain all my choices, especially those that differ from traditions that do not seem to me to fit a cogent itinerary; but I will only mention a few rejected hypotheses, for they are countless. And as we go along, I will review the principal episodes of *The Odyssey*, at the same time telling the story of my own small adventures, always remembering that for me as for Ulysses, memory is a phenomenon of love and of her sister, hatred. We all tend to forget that of which we are less fond unless, of course, we hate it. I have found this fact progressively more evident in the writings of Columbus, culminating in the *lettera rarissima* he wrote at the end of his last voyage.

Finally, in the last chapter I will present my conclusions concerning Homer and his poem, for I think by then that you, reader, will agree with me that enough data will have been brought together to present a new and reasonable answer to the old Homeric question. If my theories convince you, my labors will be more than amply rewarded; but even should they not, if our flight leads you to reread Homer, to propose your own hypotheses, and to discover again that there is no end to the ever-increasing joy the Homeric epics can provide, I will by no means have labored in vain. For none can labor in vain who loves his work even more than its goal.

NOTES ON THE
WORLD OF ULYSSES

Tablets and Takeoff

Gods and Men

Elements and Ships

Women and Wealth

TABLETS AND TAKEOFF

Lita and I sat on the balcony of the old house in Cadaqués, overlooking the bay to our right, and listened to the Mediterranean lapping at the peeling arches that support the part of the house that overhangs the water. To our left, fishermen's houses rose on top of one another in a white crescent, crowned by the huge gray church. They seemed to enclose a crystal sphere of space, through which the swallows chased each other with childlike screams, swooping smoothly and turning sharp corners in the air. *El gargal,*[1] the Greek wind, nudged small waves onto the pebbly beach, and as the evening tactfully displaced the day, the rounded boats began to arrive, and their crews pulled them laboriously onto the beach until they filled it completely.

My thoughts turned first downwind toward our other home, the Caribbean, then veered upwind toward the Mediterranean, where Ulysses had so many times beached his twelve black-prowed ships in just such a twilight as this, under the gaze of yet another god, nymph, or monster. And into my mind, becalmed, my old dream sailed like an evening caravel into a quiet port, its crew intoning the Salve Regina: to follow from the air Ulysses' travels just as I had helped trace those of Columbus, a dream kept alive by my many happy rereadings of *The Odyssey*, and of the works of those who had begun to piece together the web of truth behind the poetry, a web almost as often woven and undone as Penelope's. So I turned to reading about the latest and oldest picture of the world of Ulysses, contained in the Mycenaean tablets deciphered only twenty years ago by the English architect Michael Ventris, whose feat confounded the experts and completed the Mycenaean tripod on which

1. *Gregale* in Italian, the northeaster.

our knowledge of the Heroic World stands; Homeric tradition, archaeology, and now the written record.

The story of this "tripod" runs something like this: Up to the nineteenth century, most historians based their estimate of the "prehistory" of Greece on Homer as a myth, until in 1876 a visionary German amateur and genius, Heinrich Schliemann, began his archaeological pursuit of Homer toward Troy and Mykene. In 1890 he died alone in Italy, having run through two fortunes, two wives, and the patience of many experts and governments. But he had "gazed upon the face of Agamemnon," as he is supposed to have cabled the Kaiser, and his spade uncovered a whole civilization and helped restore the world's faith in the truth of *The Iliad* and *The Odyssey*. In one respect, however, he had failed: he had found no sample of the writing of a culture that could hardly have been illiterate, and he had not obtained permission to excavate at Knossos, where the tablets waited.

Toward the end of the century a proud professional, Sir Arthur Evans, keeper of the Ashmolean Museum at Oxford, began to study the first samples of writing of the period, found on seal-stones and pottery, and apparently more related to Hittite hieroglyphs than to the Greek world of Mykene. But once again Homer led the way, this time to Crete; and early in this century Evans began his self-confident reconstruction of the palace at Knossos. In the process he found what had evaded Schliemann: hundreds of clay tablets inscribed in two successive forms of writing, both distinct from the Hittite, which he called "Linear-A" and "Linear-B." Their language he assumed to be Cretan, or Minoan, as distinct from Greek.

In the 1940s, still following Homer, Carl Blegen of Cincinnati, with a Greco-American team, pushed the trail one stage further when he uncovered Nestor's palace at Ano-Englianos near Pylos on the Bay of Navarino, the same historic bay in which the ancient Athenians defeated the Spartans, and the nineteenth-century Europeans the Turks. Here Linear-B tablets appeared for the first time on the continent, filed by the hundreds in a great archive, where they had apparently been kept in wooden chests as at Knossos. And a little later a British team under A. J. B. Wace found Linear-B tablets at Mykene, and established that they had been preserved, ironically, by the great series of fires that destroyed the palaces between 1400 and 1200 B.C., baking the tablets hard.

In the meantime, shortly before the First World War, an English schoolboy named Michael Ventris heard Evans' lecture, "The Minoan World," and could not forget it. In 1950 Ventris published what came to be known as "The Mid-Century Report." This summary of the replies of leading authorities to a questionnaire prepared by Ventris revealed that the language of the tablets still remained a mystery, and that the experts still generally believed that the mainland Mycenaeans had been conquered by the Cretans, who had brought their Minoan language with them. This was a strangely anti-Homeric assumption for a man like Evans, whose great discoveries had been made in the bard's footsteps. *The Iliad* clearly states that King Idomeneus of Crete contributed eighty ships to Agamemnon's expedition against Troy, which confirms his feudal allegiance to Mykene, and not the reverse.

Wace had indeed cast doubts on this dominance of the legend of the Minotaur over the historical poems of Homer, doubts that at one stage even cost him his post as head of the British School at Athens. But it remained for Ventris and his collaborator, Dr. John Chadwick, the Cambridge linguist, to apply scientific systems of code-breaking to the tablets, and to prove that their language was Greek after all. Homer was once again vindicated as a historian, but not until several years of vicious attacks by men like Beattie, Chadwick's old teacher, who were finally silenced when Ventris's alphabet withstood the test of fitting subsequent finds of tablets, principally the famous Tripod Tablet from Pylos.

Ventris died in 1956, before he was thirty-five years old, but the historical revolution he started continues to this day, as the belief gains ground that it was the Mycenaeans who conquered Crete, bringing *their* language with them, and that the series of fires that finally destroyed their world may have been caused by the invasion from the sea that the Pylians of the tablets were apparently preparing to resist, even as the fortifications of Mykene and of Tiryns were being strengthened and extended to include water supplies. Could the invaders have been the Dorians, and could the Dorians have been the legendary "Peoples of the Sea" whose growing aggressiveness coincided with the end of the Hittites, and who were finally stopped in Egypt under Ramses III? Could they even have been the mythical "Sons of Herakles," who waited so long to wreak vengeance upon the sons of Neleus and his son Nestor of Pylos, Ulysses' friend? Or is it more probable that the Peoples of the Sea were the Mycenaeans themselves, attacking each other and the rest of the world like wandering Samurai once their feudal system broke down, perhaps because of the lords' too-long absence at Troy? According to this hypothesis the Great Peace mentioned by Homer at the end of *The Odyssey* would be *Pax Doriana*.

All these questions merit reading many other books besides this one. Yet, whatever the answers, the tablets have given us a complete bureaucratic record of the oarsmen, artisans, women, children, ship's stores, furniture, and rations of the Mycenaean world, reminiscent in their meticulous detail of the Spanish archives of Simancas and of the Indies, and as different from poetry as bones are from flesh, but equally essential. They contain the first written record of the civilization described by Homer, and, as archaeology continues to uncover objects from both worlds, new evidence still flows into the discussion of the similarities and differences between the world of the tablets and that of the poet.

For me, the similarities have already carried the day. I will refer to them as my story unfolds, but, from the start, one thing struck me particularly, leaving a question at the back of my mind that jolted to the surface when navigational considerations brought me to the same line of thought. Linear-A has not yet been completely deciphered, but, as a writing system, its similarity to the Hittite hieroglyphics that preceded it, and to Linear-B, which succeeded it, seems clear. Here is one example: [2]

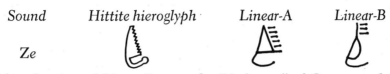

Sound	Hittite hieroglyph	Linear-A	Linear-B
Ze			

After the time of Linear-B came the "dark ages" of Greece, and then the appearance of the classic Greek alphabet, based on that of the Phoenicians. But there is one exceptional case, that of the Cypriots, who in many ways seem to have been the "ultraconservatives" of the Greek world. Until classical times, their language, Arkadio-Cypriot, remained almost identical to that of the Mycenaean tablets, and had much in common with Aeolic. More surprising still, even when the rest of the Greek world had adopted the alphabet originated in Phoenicia, so close to Cyprus, the Cypriots continued to use a syllabic writing strikingly similar to Linear-A and Linear-B. And inscriptions and coins have shown that this syllabic writing of Cyprus was continually in use at least from the seventh to the second century B.C., and it is generally agreed that it must be much older.

Here are some examples: [3]

Sound	Cypriot	Linear-B
Da	⊢	⊢
Na	⊤	Ῡ
Pa	‡	‡
Po	ς	𝄬

2. Leonard R. Palmer (see Bibliography).
3. For an incomparably more learned discussion of these alphabets, read Chadwick (see Bibliography).

Sound	Cypriot	Linear-B
Se		
To		

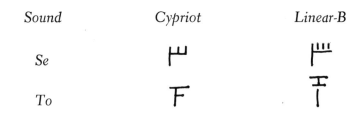

Now, the language of the Cypriot inscriptions was not proved to be Greek until almost the same year Schliemann started his archaeological pursuit of Homer. Thus all these coincidences have become apparent only in the twentieth century. And the question still stuck in my mind: remembering that Pylians migrated to Cyprus as well as to Athens and Ionia after the Dorian invasion, might not a Cypriot Homer of the eighth century B.C. have been able to read the clay tablets of Pylos? [4]

I will return to the date of Homer and to the riddle of his origin in my last chapter, after we have retraced his *Odyssey* and seen that it reserves a special place for Cyprus and even for its stars. But the fact is that on the terrace of the old house at Cadaqués that summer evening, the record of the tablets became the last breath of the "Greek wind" that was needed to launch our airborne Odyssey. And I started, as every good mariner must, with a question in my mind.

So it was that Lita and I came to be sitting for the third day at Cointrin Airport in Geneva, waiting for the weather to clear, with our new *Oh Papa* full of gas and loaded with photographic gear and with luggage, which in this case ranged from life jackets to Lita's new wig, acquired to supplant her hairdresser but, in the end, never used. Fortunately, neither were the life jackets. Geneva's wind *la bise* had held us for three days under a solid cover of cloud stretching all the way to the Mediterranean, which was hardly the setting in which to begin our

---

4. Paper was not imported into Greece until much later, and then from Biblos (today in Lebanon), whence it took its Greek name ("papyrus" being Egyptian), so that even Homer, if he wrote down *The Odyssey*, must have done so on leather scrolls, or "diphtherai."

photographic flight into antiquity. But today "Meteo," the meteorological service, had told me that the Mediterranean was beginning to clear, and if I was willing to pierce the cloud and cross the Alps above it at about twelve thousand feet, we would be in the clear by the time we reached the French Riviera. So I filed my flight plan, filled the forms that were supposed to exempt me from gasoline taxes but did not, fired up *Oh Papa*, and climbed timidly into the cloud over Lake Geneva, confident that the sun awaited us above. After all, who was I to doubt the word of a Swiss meteorologist? My faith was soon rewarded: at exactly twelve thousand feet we left the murk, and with Mont Blanc rearing its snows through the cloud ahead of us, sailed up into the clear Alpine air to almost sixteen thousand feet.

"Unlimber your camera on that," I told Lita, "for there is nothing higher between our Andes and the Himalayas." And as we approached the peak, Lita aiming her camera, I finished trimming the plane for level flight, with its turbos compressing the thin air to the taste of its clocklike little engines. I had switched tanks and cut electric pumps, all in accordance with the short course I had been given before being "checked out" in this aircraft, which I had not previously flown. Then the right engine quit.

There was a millisecond's silence, then Lita's shutter clicked[5] and I went into my emergency routine, fighting back a strong urge to climb away from the fog-shrouded fingers of the Alps below. But my left engine took up its increased load exactly as foreseen in Mr. Piper's manual, and with an exclamation of relief I turned toward the Rhône Valley, beyond the mountains to our right. As soon as I knew we could make it, I tried the dead engine again, and after a couple of tries it started.

When we landed at Nice I found that there were no maintenance facilities for private planes. So I looked over the offending engine, and seeing no obvious trouble, phoned Geneva and was told that this some-

5. See photo page 20.

Emergency over the Alps

times happened on early models if, after switching tanks, one turned off the fuel pumps before they had had time to digest the air lock that sometimes formed. "But they always start again," Geneva added, which seemed a doubtful consolation to Lita. Finally I slept on the matter and decided to take off in the morning on our first Mediterranean leg toward Corsica, simply leaving the electric fuel pumps on a little longer next time. Our expedition had started on a proper note of excitement, and we had survived without difficulty, thanks perhaps to the protection of some guardian angel who remembered in time his distant kinship to Athena, Ulysses' protector.

Before proceeding any further with our tale, I must attempt a few notes on the world into which we are about to fly, or at least on the form it has taken in my mind through these years of familiarity aloft, afloat, and in the library. Although there is, of course, no substitute for a careful reading of Homer's poems themselves, the studious reader can dedicate a lifetime to assimilating any number of different views of this ancient world. My purpose here is merely to organize very briefly my own view of what is known of the Mycenaeans, as they are now called (after the name of Agamemnon's capital city), or the Acheans or Argives, as they are interchangeably called by Homer, and so to establish a background for my navigational observations.

GODS AND MEN

Homer's gods are easy to understand but difficult to explain—easy to understand as soon as one has spent some time with the poems, but difficult to explain because the very word *god* obstructs the explanation in modern terms. The fact is that the gods of the Mycenaeans are not otherworldly spirits but an integral part of Mycenaean society, an essentially feudal society in which everyone is immediately subject to a superior or master of an inferior. There are servants, squires, chieftains, kings, and overlords; and within this framework one might do better to speak of "superlords" than of gods.

That this world is feudal seems clear in Homer, where Echepolus of Sikyon escapes service at Troy by giving Agamemnon a mare named Aithe ("Blaze"), while Euchenor of Corinth, on the contrary, goes to Troy to avoid a fine. These are typical facts of feudal life, where property and power depend on service. And Agamemnon, in order to indemnify Achilles, promises not only treasure and his own daughter in marriage, but also seven cities, all situated in lands in the domain of Nestor or of Menelaos, who in his turn says of Ulysses: "If Providence had allowed us to sail home together from Troy, I'd have emptied one of the towns in my own dominions and given it to him to live in. I'd have built him a house and transplanted him from Ithaka with all his possessions and his people too."[1] All these are attitudes typical of feudal overlords, and the picture is confirmed by the tablets, where the whole structure of land tenure runs clearly down from "Wanax," the king, to the common man, through a series of intermediate classes whose rights and obligations appear to be established by mutual agreement.

Since they form part of a tightly knit hierarchy, the Mycenaeans' gods, or superlords, are ever present to illuminate everyday things like bread and wine and death with that transcendence necessary to sanity which we so lack today, though Christ tried to give it back to us. There is no question as to the gods' existence: the only question concerns their possible behavior, for they are imperfect gods, and therefore quite real.

One might conjecture that whereas we have to make do with an imperfect faith in a perfect God, the Mycenaeans were more comfortable with their perfect faith in imperfect gods, for it is always difficult to seek perfection without first making one's peace with imperfection. A good example of the gods' almost human imperfection is their favoritism, which Nestor has in mind when he says that he never saw such open affection and championship as that of Pallas Athena for Ulysses; and when Athena, who has accompanied Telemachos to Nestor's palace,

i. These minor Roman numerals refer to Quotations from *The Odyssey*, page 177.

takes the form of a sea eagle and flies from Pylos beach, he notes that Telemachos takes after his father in enjoying her partisanship. No one can doubt this episode who, like me, has followed a pair of eagles down the god-infested canyons of Delphi as they "glided down the wind with outstretched pinions, wing to wing." [ii]

These imperfect superlords act exactly as such, their always human reactions simply magnified by their wonderful powers, which, though almost unlimited by the laws of Nature, are often very much limited by the desires and actions of another god. This situation has quite distinct advantages, not the least of which is that the gods, in order to avoid chaos, must enter into contracts or covenants not only with each other, but also with men, thus laying the foundation for all subsequent justice by simple *do ut des*.

At the very beginning of *The Odyssey*, Zeus, the father of them all, complains that men insist on blaming the gods for all the evils that obviously result from man's own foolish actions, and Homer's humans do, in fact, derive a very comforting sense of justification from blaming their superiors. The prime example of this is not Ulysses—for though he also blames all his misfortunes on the wrath of Poseidon, he still admits that their source lies in his own actions—but that most successful of cuckolds, Menelaos, whom we find long after Troy, honored, wealthy, and satisfied in the company of his Helen, whose expensive infidelity he has managed to blame entirely on the gods, who "momentarily blinded her better judgment."

This situation, in which men live according to a series of bilateral agreements and simply pay the price whenever an agreement is broken, or in the last resort blame the gods, leads to a life where man can afford to live by manners rather than by morals, and be virtuous and noble for reasons more sensible than the nagging avoidance of a sense of guilt. Revenge, not guilt, is to be avoided, and the punishment meted out by authority is in fact quite lenient. One has the feeling that since no more than a bilateral contract has been broken, a third party such as the State has little if any business in intervening. A murderer, for example, can at most be fined or exiled by the State; but if he is caught by the injured family, revenge is likely to be capital, and will be accepted as justice by society. But the principal moderator of behavior is still good manners. Thus, when Noemon, having lent his ship to Telemachos, is accused by Antinoös, "fuming with indignation, his heart seething with black passion, his eyes like pods of flame," Noemon's defense is simple: how could he refuse "a man of Telemachos' standing with so much trouble on his mind"? [iii] All this might profitably be remembered in the twentieth century, which seems to be throwing morals out the window without caring that manners have gone before; the young bent on replacing manners with style, the old, morals with money.

In any case, manners are most important, as young Navsikaa shows when she finds Ulysses shipwrecked and naked, and after listening to him exclaims: "Sir, your manners show that you are no rascal and no fool"; [iv] and she is right, for the poet makes clear that Ulysses' greatest virtue is his capacity for fooling gods as well as men, while never being fooled himself.

So, with the gods, a Mycenaean minds his manners by offering the proper sacrifices at the proper times, which is pleasant because these ceremonies always include good food and drink for all. The word *sacrifice* simply means "to make sacred," and can apply as much to pleasure as to pain, which makes it significant that the ancients, while sacrificing, usually thought more of the first, while we think instinctively of the second. He minds his manners with his fellow men by willing observance of the laws of hospitality, which also assume a joyously sacramental value because all strangers are wards of Zeus; by respecting his neighbor's property, which includes his wife and slaves; and by giving proper burial so that the dead may expediently cross the River into Hades. And Hades, though by no means a desirable abode, appears preferable to wandering alone in the ghostly purgatory that awaits those over whose bodies the proper rites have not been performed.

The burial customs of the Mycenaean world are important to us, not only because they figure so prominently in both *The Iliad* and *The Odyssey*, but because the Mycenaeans have become identified as builders of great mounds, or Tholos ("beehive") tombs,[6] although earlier they used simpler shaft graves such as those discovered by Schliemann at Mykene. The main thing is that they did not cremate their dead, which has served to differentiate them from their enemies. To this rule there is one exception of which much has been made, but its explanation seems quite simple. At the close of *The Iliad*, Achilles organizes the solemn cremation, not burial, of his beloved Patroklos, though he deals shamefully with the body of Trojan Hector, a breach of manners for which he will pay dearly. (Hector's slaying itself will be considered a normal revenge.) The explanation of this Mycenaean cremation is that proper burial in a foreign land is useless, for the purpose of ceremonial burial is honor, which the body of a Mycenaean hero will not for long enjoy if buried in the land of his enemies. However, the first expeditionary to die on the way back from Troy is Phrontis, Menelaos' helmsman, who is *buried* with full honors right where he dies in Attica, though this means delaying the fleet at least a full day at Cape Sounion, and results in a much more serious delay when half the fleet is blown to Crete and the other half to Egypt. On the other hand Elpenor, in Hades, begs Ulysses to give him decent "burial" by burning him with his arms and building him a mound, which Ulysses does as soon as he returns to foreign Aiaia where Elpenor lies dead. Incidentally, it seems to me that Phrontis' grave on Sounion, together with Ulysses' palace on Ithaka, must soon be found by the archaeologists, as has so much else out of Homer and the tablets.

But to return to the gods, in Homer they seem to have two ways of communicating with men: when they wish to be equivocal they use omens and signs such as bird lore; but when they wish to be clearly un-

6. See photo page 26.

Tholos Tombs at Mykene

derstood they simply disguise themselves as men, and speak. This explains why their pronouncements are sometimes taken seriously and sometimes not, as shown by one suitor's answer to Halisethes the soothsayer, at the assembly called by Telemachos to regain control of his own palace: "Plenty of birds go about their business in the sunny sky, but not every one has a meaning."ᵛ Meaningful or not, the twentieth century seems to miss this direct communication with Heaven, and the passion of today's Greeks for using white-painted stones to inscribe names or prayers on mountainsides in letters forty feet high appears to me a protest to the gods for having fallen silent. But Mycenaeans, always sure of a hearing, washed their hands in the surf and lifted them up in solitary prayer like Telemachos, or filled a basket with sacrificial grain and reminded the gods of past sacrifices, like Penelope praying for her son when she learned he was to be ambushed by the suitors. Or, if the occasion warranted it, they offered a great sacrifice such as Nestor's, an episode that surely merits full quotation:

They all hurried off to carry out his orders. The heifer was brought in from the meadows; Prince Telemachus' crew came up from his good ship; and the smith arrived, equipped with the tools of his trade, the anvil, the hammer, and the sturdy tongs he used for working gold. Athene too attended to accept the sacrifice. Then Nestor the old charioteer gave out the gold, which the smith worked into foil and laid round the heifer's horns by way of embellishment to please the goddess' eye. Next Stratius and Echephron led the heifer forward by the horns, and Aretus came out from the store-room, carrying in his right hand a flowered bowl of lustral water for their use, and in the other a basket with the barley-corns, while the stalwart Thrasymedes, gripping a sharp axe, stood by to cut the victim down, and Perseus held the dish to catch its blood.

The old charioteer Nestor now started the ritual with the lustral water and the scattered grain, and offered up his earnest prayers to Athene as he began the sacrifice by throwing a lock from the victim's head on the fire.

When they had made their petitions and sprinkled the barley-corns, Nestor's son Thrasymedes stepped boldly up and struck. The axe cut through the tendons of the heifer's neck and she collapsed. At this, the women raised their cry, Nestor's daughters and his sons' wives, and his loyal consort Eurydice, Clymenus' eldest daughter. But the men lifted the heifer's head from the trodden earth and held it up while the captain Peisistratus cut its throat. When the dark blood had gushed out and life had left the heifer's bones, they swiftly dismembered the carcass, cut slices off the thighs in ceremonial fashion, wrapped them in folds of fat and laid raw meat above them. These pieces the venerable king burnt on the faggots, while he sprinkled red wine over the flames, and the young men gathered round with five-pronged forks in their hands. When the thighs were burnt up and they had tasted the inner parts, they carved the rest into small pieces, pierced them with skewers and held the sharp ends of the spits to the fire till all was roasted. . . .

When they had roasted the outer flesh and drawn it off the skewers, they took their seats at table, with men of gentle birth to wait on them and fill their golden cups with wine.[vi]

This sacrifice near the sea is offered to Poseidon. As is proper in a feudal pantheon like the Mycenaeans', each of the gods has his domain: Zeus presides in Olympos, while his brother Poseidon dominates the sea, and Hades rules the realm of the dead. Earth seems to be common ground, though each island, river, or cave has its own minor deity or nymph to whom the locals pay homage. But I will not here go into the names and relationships of all the gods, except to point out that those who appear in the tablets correspond so closely to Homer's and to the Mycenaeans' that Palmer quotes the comment of an Italian scholar: "*E troppo bello!*" But one detail is particularly interesting: The preponderance in the Pylian tablets of Poseidon and of Potnia, the queen, recalls the evidence which seems to show that the cult of Poseidon reached the Mycenaeans from the East via Cyprus, where the cult of Wanassa, the queen, continued until after the time of Homer. But to all of this I will return in Chapter V, when I make my case for a Cypriot Homer.

ELEMENTS AND SHIPS

After ten years at Troy, Ulysses seems to have been the principal architect of its horse-borne destruction, for which he was rewarded with the
curse of Cassandra, one of the causes of his subsequent woes.

Immediately after their victory, King Agamemnon and his brother,
red-haired Menelaos, Helen's husband, quarreled over the return schedule. Worse, they did so in the evening in front of the assembled troops,
when most of them had done justice to their ration of wine and were
therefore no longer very rational. The debate became a shambles, and the
royal brothers parted company. Running his ships down into the tranquil
sea "after stowing his loot and his captive women with their girdles
round their hips," [vii] Menelaos set sail for nearby Tenedos Island and
home, with Ulysses among his followers, while Agamemnon and the rest
of the army remained on the Trojan plain to sacrifice to the gods before
departing. In the long run Menelaos seems to have been right, for years
later we meet him through Telemachos, happily feasting with his fair
Helen among the splendors of Sparta, while Agamemnon rots in his
grave, sent there by his wife Klytaimnestra and her lover Aigisthos. But
in the short run Agamemnon was right, for thanks to his sacrifice the
gods gave him safe passage home, while Menelaos and his followers were
scattered by the great storm. So it is always with the favor of the gods:
its apparent value depends upon where and when it is measured, and
only for a very privileged few does the wheel of fortune cease to turn in
life, though cease it must for each in death.

But Ulysses, as usual, obeyed no one but himself, first following
Menelaos to Tenedos where they sacrificed to the gods, then doubling
back to rejoin Agamemnon, before finally setting off alone with his own
squadron to sack Ismaros, the city of the Kikones, and barely escaping

their vengeance to proceed to Cape Malea, where his Odyssey really begins. And it is between Troy and Malea that we begin to find what we need in order to commence our re-exploration of the world of *The Odyssey*. First of all, a description of the performance of the type of ship that will carry Ulysses to the limits of the known world and beyond, and then something about the elements of that world itself. Let Nestor speak:

Our ships went well, for luckily no swell was running and the sea was smooth. We soon made Tenedos, and there, all agog to be home, we sacrificed to the gods. But Zeus had no intention of letting us get home so soon, and for his own cruel purposes he set us all at loggerheads once more. As a result, one squadron swung the curved prows of their vessels round and turned back in their tracks. It was the followers of Odysseus, that wise and subtle king, who thus saw fit to renew their allegiance to Agamemnon son of Atreus. But I, well aware of the god's sinister designs, fled on with the massed ships that formed my company. Warlike Diomedes did the same, bringing his party with him, and late in our wake red-haired Menelaus followed too. He caught us up in Lesbos, where we were hesitating whether to choose the long passage outside the rugged coast of Chios and by way of Psyria, keeping that island on our left, or to sail inside Chios past the windy heights of Mimas. In this dilemma we prayed for a sign, and heaven made it clear that we should cut straight across the open sea to Euboea to get out of harm's way as quickly as possible. A whistling wind blew up, and our ships made splendid running down the highways of the fish, reaching Geraestus in the night. And many a bull's thigh we laid on Poseidon's altar after spanning that weary stretch of water.

It was on the fourth day that the company of Diomedes the tamer of horses brought their fine craft to anchor in Argos. But I held on for Pylos, and the breeze never dropped from the moment when by god's will it had begun to blow....[viii]

But when we were abreast of the sacred cape of Sunion where Attica juts out into the sea, Phoebus Apollo let fly his gentle darts at Menelaus' helmsman and struck him dead, with the steering-oar of the running ship in his hands.

This man Phrontis son of Onetor had been the world's best steersman in a gale, and Menelaus, though anxious to proceed, was detained at Sunion till he could bury his comrade with the proper rites. But when he too had got away over the wine-dark sea in those great ships of his and had run as far as the steep bluff of Malea, Zeus, who is always on the watch, took it into his head to give them a rough time, and sent them a howling gale with giant waves as massive and as high as mountains. Then and there he split the fleet into two parts, one of which he drove toward Crete and the Cydonian settlements on the River Iardanus. Now where the lands of Gortyn end, out in the misty sea, there is a smooth rock that falls abruptly to the water, and the south-westerly gales drive the great rollers against a headland to the left, in towards Phaestos, with nothing but this puny reef to keep their violence in check. It was here that the one party made their landfall. The crews by a hair's breadth escaped destruction; their ships were splintered on the rocks by the fury of the seas. Meanwhile Menelaus with the remaining five vessels of his blue-prowed fleet was driven on by wind and wave to Egypt.[ix]

These are the words of the oldest and wisest of Mycenaean kings, who has reigned through three generations, and the best storyteller to boot. They merit careful study, for from them we can learn a good deal about the Mycenaeans' sailing methods, about the speed of their ships, and about the general meteorological conditions that prevailed about the time Ulysses must have reached Cape Malea, thence to be blown from the familiar world.

The first part of Nestor's story was told to Telemachos when he visited the old king at Pylos in search of news of Ulysses. And Telemachos sailed to Pylos from Ithaka in one long night, with a favorable wind brought by Athena, who accompanied him under the guise of Mentor. Now the distance from Ithaka to Pylos is much the same as the distance from Lesbos to Geraistos in Euboia, about one hundred nautical miles; and each distance was covered—the former by Nestor, Menelaos, and Diomedes and the latter by Telemachos and Athena—in one night, each with a favorable wind. So we have our first precise piece of information about the type of ships with which we have to deal: they cover one hundred nautical miles in about twelve hours with a favorable wind—that is, eight knots across open water—which is quite a reasonable conclusion.[7]

But this is by no means the way the Mycenaeans normally sail. As Nestor's doubts well show, they prefer to follow the coast by day and in the summer, probably averaging about four knots, a speed that is confirmed by the oldest of sailing directions, to which I will refer in the next chapter, that of Scylax, who figures five hundred stadia a day. The night, the winter, and the open sea are to be avoided whenever possible. Finally, if Ulysses' ships make eight knots sailing before a favorable wind, they probably make no more than two knots when being blown unwillingly off course with the sail down, which happens uncomfortably often in *The Odyssey*. Note that I speak only of sailing with the wind, for the Mycenaeans certainly could get no closer to the wind than a modern Chinese junk, and if their course lay upwind, they would either row if the wind allowed it, or wait out the wind on the nearest beach or at anchor. *Oh Papa*, incidentally, does about one hundred and eighty knots!

There are remarkably few good contemporary representations of Mycenaean or Cretan ships. A Mycenaean wreck has indeed been found, and I will refer to its details in Chapter IV, but no authentic Cretan wreck has ever turned up. This may be because no one has searched with modern means for remains of the fleet that is supposed to have dominated the eastern Mediterranean and should therefore not have disappeared without a trace.[8] But in Homer the ships themselves are fairly well described. Telemachos' has twenty oars, and Antilochos' too, but there is frequent reference to "big" ships, while the Pylian tablets, referring to preparations for war, list forty men per ship. Now the Phaiak-

7. See charts pages 33 and 35. Palmer (see Bibliography) goes into the subject of distances and speeds quite thoroughly.

8. When I pointed this out to Najar and Dumas during our Jamaican search for Columbus's last caravels, they immediately mounted an expedition to Crete, though I also suggested the possibility that the Cretans may not have been masters of a powerful fleet at all.

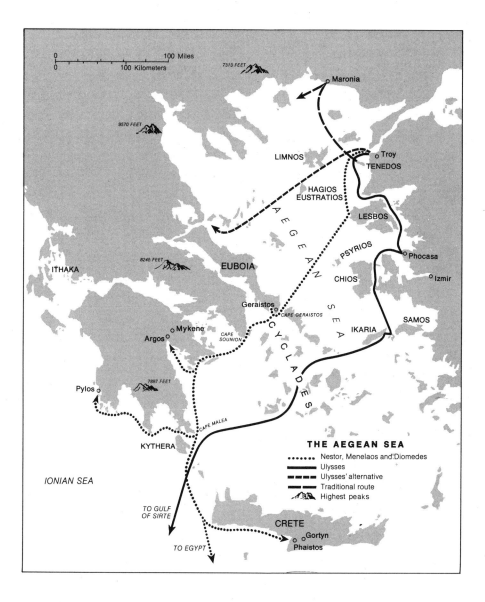

THE AEGEAN SEA

Nestor, Menelaos and Diomedes ········
Ulysses ———
Ulysses' alternative – – –
Traditional route — —
Highest peaks 🏔

100 Miles
100 Kilometers

7313 FEET

Maronia

9570 FEET

LIMNOS

Troy
TENEDOS

HAGIOS
EUSTRATIOS

LESBOS

PSYRIOS

Phocasa

Izmir

ITHAKA

8245 FEET

EUBOIA

CHIOS

A E G E A N

Geraistos
CAPE GERAISTOS

S E A

SAMOS

IKARIA

Mykene
Argos

CAPE
SOUNION

C Y C L A D E S

7897 FEET

Pylos

CAPE MALEA

KYTHERA

IONIAN SEA

TO GULF
OF SIRTE

CRETE
Gortyn
Phaistos

TO EGYPT

33

ians' ship, which finally brings Ulysses home, carries forty-five oars, so we can assume that Achean ships carried between twenty and forty-five oarsmen, the shorter and beamier being merchant ships, and the longer and narrower (for speed), warships. In *The Odyssey*, these ships carry wine in jars and barley meal in "well-sewn skins," all of which is confirmed by the tablets.

The ships are run up on the beach at night whenever possible, and in the morning they are run down again into the water, "gear stowed, fir mast hauled up, stept in its hollow box and made fast with stays, and oars fixed in their slings. At last the white sail is hoisted with plaited oxhide ropes," [x] exactly like those made to this day in my Colombian cattle country by cutting a spiral out of the rawhide, then twisting and stretching it to dry in the sun. When the ship is to be moored temporarily, the sail is brailed up, as at Pylos. The sails themselves are always described as white, and must have been made either of linen or of wool supported by a net, which seems to be how the Norsemen made theirs. And also like the Norsemen's, Mycenaean ships are governed with a large steering oar or "steerboard," apparent origin of the word *starboard*.

And what about the elements and the shape of the earth through which these "well-found ships" carried their captains? If it is true that Homer naturally tells his story in a "pictorial" manner, wherein lies much of its charm, it is also true that his mental picture of the world and its elements definitely appears to be more literary than pictorial. These are subjects too large to be envisioned without a "cartographic mentality," something that did not become common until very much later, though we do have a Babylonian clay map of the fourth millennium B.C.,[9] and Anaximander of Miletus and others made maps in the sixth century B.C. Geography remained a branch of philosophy at least until the time of Ptolemy in the second century A.D., and this explains why each Homeric commentarist produces his individual picture of Homer's earth, none of which seems quite satisfactory from a naviga-

9. Plate V in Bagrow (see Bibliography).

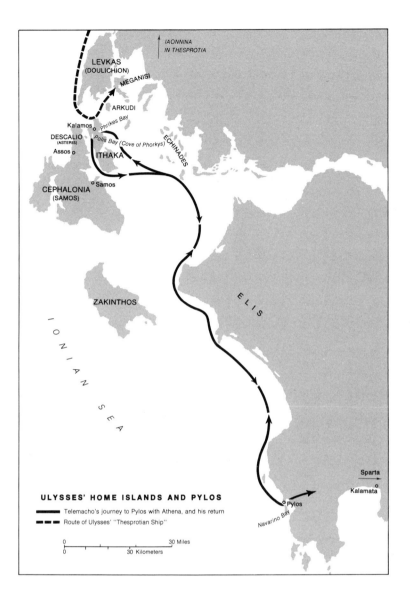

IAONNINA
IN THESPROTIA

LEVKAS
(DOULICHION)

MEGANISI

ARKUDI

Kalamos o   Phrikes Bay
DESCALIO   Polis Bay (Cove of Phorkys)
(ASTERIS)
Assos o   ITHAKA   ECHINADES

o Samos

CEPHALONIA
(SAMOS)

ZAKINTHOS

E L I S

I O N I A N   S E A

Sparta

Kalamata

o Pylos

Navarino Bay

ULYSSES' HOME ISLANDS AND PYLOS

———— Telemacho's journey to Pylos with Athena, and his return
▬ ▬ ▬ Route of Ulysses' "Thesprotian Ship"

0 ————————————— 30 Miles
0 ————————————— 30 Kilometers

tional point of view. So, unabashedly, I will set forth my own view in two diagrams, one of the winds, the other of the earth, as I translate them from Homer's beautiful but imprecise verse into our cold but measurable cartographic language.[10]

For the Acheans, the Earth is "never ending" and includes Olympos, principal home of the gods. The sea is a part of it that men use for transportation, and sea gods for habitation; the ocean, on the other hand, is "all encircling," and seems to frame a disc or globe that encompasses all of man's experience, including his gods. Out of the endless ocean, and into man's complex of land and sea, there flow two Rivers of Ocean, one from the west, where the sun sets and where men go after death, and one from the east, where lie the Elysian Fields and where the day is born. I do not hesitate to identify these two Rivers of Ocean with the Straits of Gibraltar to the west, and with the Bosphorus to the east. *The Iliad* speaks clearly of "crossing the Ocean Stream to reach the Ethiopians," and of a dead man disappearing into the "western gloom," thus apparently situating Hades beyond Gibraltar, which, of the two rivers, is the one that concerns us here. The currents of the rivers—that of the western river is carefully described in *The Odyssey*—correspond exactly to those that flow to this day, because the Mediterranean's sun evaporates far more water than its few great rivers are able to replace, a condition that must have been even more notorious before the opening of Suez, and to which I will refer in Chapter III. The idea that Paradise lies to the east and Doom to the west seems to have lasted until the Renaissance, for Columbus sailed west to reach the Far East, and said he found Paradise in Paria, today's Venezuela.

As to winds, directions, currents, and distances, Mycenaean notions of the first were much more personal than ours, and much vaguer as to the others. Winds were known by name, as they are to this day all over

10. See pages 37 and 39.

← Prevailing currents

ALL - ENCIRCLING OCEAN

NEVER - ENDING EARTH

ELYSIAN RIVER OF OCEAN

Bosporus

LAISTRYGONES

OLYMPOS

WESTERN RIVER OF OCEAN

S E A

HADES

Gibraltar

ETHIOPIANS

NEVER - ENDING EARTH

LOTOPHAGI

ALL - ENCIRCLING OCEAN

the Mediterranean,[11] and not by their directions. They were generally recognized by their personality, that is to say by their temperature, their constancy, their smell, their taste, and even their voice. Here again Catalan Cadaqués is Greek, as is the color of its skies, rocks, and waters, for, upon awakening, the locals need not open their windows to tell which wind is blowing: they easily recognize the way each speaks to the pebbles on the beach. Like people, the Mycenaeans' winds had humors good and bad. For example, Boreas, today's *meltemi*, brought and brings good weather in summer and bad in winter; and winds have humors to this day, for even the reliable Swiss prefer to commit their crimes of passion under the influence of the southerly *foehn*, first cousin to the Catalans' *garbí* or the Italians' *sirocco*, both destroyers of domestic peace. Even today each wind tends to be true to its inborn character: The *tramontana* (north-northeast), for example, is a big cat, which often puts out its paw in the form of a lenticular cloud, to play with its prey before leaping out of the north like a leopard, and has more than once dunked your author, sailing dinghy and all. "*Saltó la tramontana*," say the fishermen: "tramontana has jumped."

Consequently, though *The Iliad* does speak of Boreas in the north, Zephyr in the west, and Notos in the South, and in our reading of Homer we must situate each wind in its proper home quarter, in my opinion we must also give it about 45 degrees leeway, for we are dealing with a living personality, and not with a fixed point on the compass. Actually, we will be taking into account only the truly great winds, which, it is reasonable to suppose, have not changed significantly since the days of Ulysses.

Currents, on the other hand, are not very strong in the Mediterranean. The Mycenaeans certainly knew them in some channels where they were worth using, notably the Rivers of Ocean, but otherwise gave them no identity. Directions, in turn, were judged either by the winds they

11. See chart page 39.

HOMER'S WINDS AND THEIR MODERN NAMES

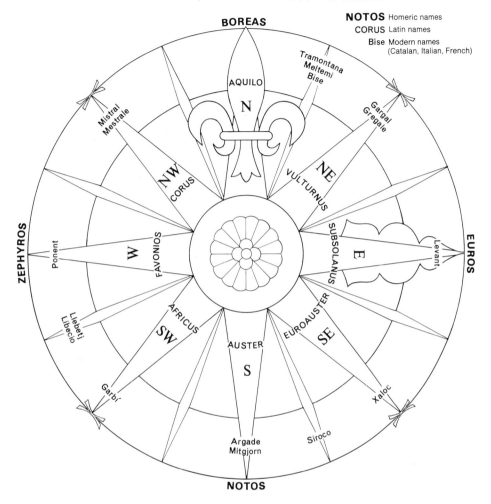

NOTOS Homeric names
CORUS Latin names
Bise Modern names
(Catalan, Italian, French)

harbored [12] or by sunrise and sunset and by the stars at night. The Bear, for example, circled the north, where Boreas dwelt, whereas Orion was always in the south, the home of Notos; and the Pleiades and Arcturus (in Boötes) chased each other from east to west, hunting grounds of Euros and Zephyr respectively. But Homer's stars are the subject of Chapter V, and I will not at this stage give them more attention.

The durations of the various "legs" of the Odyssey deserve special mention, for much has been made of them. It seems obvious that their general proportions must be respected, and that a crossing of eighteen days and nights must in fact be longer than one of three; but I do not agree to the careful multiplication of estimated speeds by the durations given in *The Odyssey*, a calculation that has fascinated many commentators, first of all because speed estimates, including my own, are too inaccurate, but more importantly because I am convinced that the durations given are mostly based on mankind's ancient magic numbers, multiples of 3 or 7, 3 being the first symmetrical number, and 7 the number of the days between the half-moon and the full, the most basic observable number outside man himself. These numbers have always been echoed by the seven stars of the Great Bear, the seven colors of the rainbow, the seven notes of the scale, the Seven Wonders of the World, as well as by the Trinity, and the common use of the "dozen" and "half-dozen." So I think *The Odyssey*, where even the dead are most often "six from each ship," is no exception.

WOMEN AND WEALTH

To the Mycenaeans, women are a form of wealth. Troy is supposedly attacked because Paris has abducted Helen, and the whole of *The Iliad*

---

12. *Lebecio, tramontana,* and *mestro,* the names of the southwest, northeast, northwest winds respectively, are still used to describe both winds and directions by Michele de Cuneo de Savona, who accompanied Columbus on his second voyage, in his famous letter of 1495 to Annari.

is based on the wrath of Achilles, who quarrels with Agamemnon over a captured slave girl. But at the same time those women they choose for wives, and to whom they are "united by the gods" (the phrase is Menelaos'), immediately assume the greatest importance, not only as pillars of the family, an institution as important as the State, but also as human beings with very special qualities. Antinoös, for example, praises Penelope, whom he wishes to marry, as an "incomparable schemer with a wonderful brain," [xi] hardly the description of a piece of property. Also, these ladies' position next to their husbands at the head of the family is never overly affected by their husbands' amorous relations, or even by their own infidelities. Jealousy, of course, exists, even cutting across social barriers, as when Ulysses' father, Laertes, respects nurse Eurykleia's bed "for fear of incurring his wife's displeasure," [xii] although he has bought the nurse from her father for twenty oxen. But apart from this instance, which is perhaps old-fashioned, concubinage is accepted by wives, and, more interesting, the men do not seem to consider their spouses' adultery as the worst of offenses.

When the Mycenaean kings leave for Troy, they seem quite sure that their kingdoms will be respected, but they are obviously not so sure of their wives, for Agamemnon (unwisely) leaves a herald in charge of Klytaimnestra, while Ulysses entrusts his whole household to Mentor, ordering him to defer only to old Laertes. Even Helen is soon forgiven, nor is Paris singled out among the Trojans for a special revenge. Orestes does avenge his father, Agamemnon, after his mother, Klytaimnestra, falls into the arms of Aigisthos "eager lover, pliant lady," [xiii] but it seems clear that Orestes is avenging his father's death at the hands of Aigisthos rather than his father's honor. Even Penelope, who is often cited as the example of fidelity, practices a sort of calculated purity, not forgetting Ulysses but not dispatching the suitors either, apparently just in case. And Telemachos, when asked by Athena if he is really Ulysses' son, points out that "it is a wise son who knows his father." [xiv] Finally, even henpecked Menelaos, when Helen can give him no more children, sires

Megapenthes by a slave, and in time marries him off to Alektor's daughter, with Helen presiding at the feast. Yet, if marriage is not too strictly monogamous, it is nevertheless a very serious thing, and rich fathers give away their daughters with suitable dowries that the ladies continue to consider their own, as Penelope clearly does when she speaks of "my servant Dolios, who keeps my orchards now." [xv] And why does Telemachos not send Penelope back to Ikarios, her father, thus easily ridding himself of the suitors who are consuming his inheritance? Simply because he would have to pay back her dowry.

As for motherhood, its ways are pretty familiar. Says Penelope to the phantom of her sister Iphthime: "Now my beloved son, for whom I tremble even more than for his father, has sailed away in a great ship, a child unprepared for action or debate!" [xvi] To which Iphthime's ghost replies that Athena has sent her to reassure Penelope that she, Athena, went with him, though he is now over twenty years old. Woman talk in any century, as is Eurykleia's statement that she loves Telemachos most, because she nursed him.

So the ladies of Mykene are far from being slaves, as long as they do not become the prize of war. If taken as booty they again become a form of wealth, their rations those summarily assigned to slaves by the tablets: men, women and children in the ratio of 5:2:1, a craftsman's daily ration being roughly one quart of wheat and one quart of wine. A dramatic change from the lot of ladies like Helen, who normally join their husbands for wine after a sumptuous dinner.

And wealth itself, and luxury? In *The Odyssey*, at the court of Menelaos, young Telemachos shows his idea of luxury when he turns to his friend Peisistratos, son of Nestor, and whispers: "Look around this echoing hall, how it gleams with copper and gold, amber, silver, and ivory." [xvii] Ulysses' storeroom is a "big lofty chamber filled with gold and bronze chests of clothing, stores of fragrant oil, and, shoulder to shoulder, jars of unblended vintage wine." [xviii] But the poet describes with the greatest pleasure those signs of wealth which are made to be enjoyed almost daily, thus displaying a typically Mediterranean taste for hoarding everything of great value, and then happily enjoying the priceless gifts of everyday life. There are carved chairs covered with rugs, or inlaid easy chairs. There are always footstools and polished tables. Hands are rinsed in silver basins filled from golden jugs. Bedsteads are wooden, but doors have silver handles and their bolts are shot home with leather thongs, as in Telemachos' "lofty chamber with a clear view of all sides," where he hangs his soft tunic on a wooden peg. And when Telemachos goes to the Assembly, he carries a bronze spear, and two dogs trot beside him. Even on the beach at Pylos, where Telemachos visits Nestor, "downy fleeces" are provided on which to sit, and wine is served in a gold cup. On his arrival at Nestor's palace, "the beautiful Polycaste, King Nestor's youngest daughter, gave Telemachos his bath. When she had bathed him and anointed him with oil, she clad him in a tunic and cast a fair cloak round his shoulders, so that he stepped forth looking like one of the immortals." [xix] The tablets list no less than thirty-seven bath girls in the palace; how hospitality has declined since then! Anyhow, Telemachos sleeps in the "echoing" portico, while the old king, like his father Neleus before him, holds court on a smooth bench of white marble in front of the lofty doors.

The Pylian tablets list jugs decorated with goddesses and bulls' heads, chariot scenes and soldiers, shells, and spiral patterns. They list three-legged caldrons decorated with lynx heads and birds, and chairs made of ebony and crystal, inlaid with ivory and gold decorations representing stags' and bulls' heads, human figures and palm trees. And they list ornate footstools and tablets. So the luxury of Homer's world and that of the tablets coincide, and the wonderful thing is that it can all be seen today at the museum in Athens and at the remains of Nestor's palace at Pylos: the hearth and the bath,[13] the storerooms, the stairways, and the portico. Only the marble bench is missing, probably removed by

13. See photos pages 44 and 47.

King Nestor's Hearth at Pylos

some tourist as long-haired as Telemachos' crew or his assemblymen.

But to return to the richest court in the poem, Menelaos himself introduces it by pointing out with characteristic immodesty that it is eclipsed only by that of Zeus, whose home and belongings are everlasting, while no mortal can compete with the fortune it has taken seven years (that magic number again!) to amass and to bring home in his ships. So Helen sits at her golden spindle in her lofty, perfumed room, spinning deep violet-blue wool, next to her a workbasket of silver rimmed with gold and standing on casters, a gift from Alcandre, wife of Polybos of Thebes in Egypt, "where houses contain the greatest store of treasures." [xx] To Menelaos Polybos gave two silver baths, a pair of three-legged caldrons, and ten talents in gold. At Sparta the guests' beds are again placed in the portico, and covered with fine purple rugs, sheets and thick blankets over them. In the evening Helen wears a long robe, while in the morning Menelaos appears with a sharp sword hanging from his shoulder, and a fine pair of sandals on his "well-shaped feet."

Of all these luxuries the most important is wine, which is always shipped and stored in concentrated form, and carefully mixed with water to suit each occasion.[14] Hesiod gives us the details of the process by which the sun is used to concentrate the power of the grapes, as it still is in Germany to produce *Trockenbeerenauslese:* "In September, cut off the grape clusters, dry them for ten days and nights, cover them for five, and on the sixth drain off the gifts of joyful Dionysos." [15] Another characteristic of Ulysses' wine has survived to this day, to the discomfort of unprepared tourists who taste *retsina* and find their mouths puckering as if full of turpentine. It seems that the Mycenaeans used pine oil to coat their wine vats, and so the taste of resin became a traditional characteristic of Greek wine. In our own times when autumn comes, Greeks and tourists alike troop out of Athens, past Eleusis and on to Daphni, where

14. One cup of Maron's wine, which he kept secret from his servants, had to be mixed with twenty of water (*Odyssey* IX 210).
15. Hesiod, 609–17 (see Bibliography).

at the wine festival all taste Vino Santo from the volcanic soil of San-torin (which used to be reserved for the Czars of Russia), Moscado from Samos, Muscadet from Kephalonia, etc. There also they find out why Greek wine, unless one specifies *aresinato*, still tastes of resin long after pine oil has ceased to be used to coat the vats: on certain days, balls of pine resin are steeped in the wine for forty days to reproduce the taste of which Ulysses was so fond. This taste, which is now hardly ex-portable, created a great demand among Pharaohs and Roman Emperors for resinated wines, including the Ariusier that Aristotle loved; and I confess that the taste of resin did not prevent me from grounding myself quite happily for several days on my first flight to Athens.

It was this concentrated wine that supported the Mycenaeans' "bal-ance of payments," along with copper, swords, and daggers and the basic olive oil they exported in their famous "stirrup jars," which are now found so far afield by archaeologists. Yet oil and wine would perhaps not have been enough to buy all the gold and other precious things that had to be imported to maintain the palaces described both in Homer and in the tablets. So we turn to the tablets once more for a hint as to what else the Mycenaeans could have exported that the archaeologists might not have found, and the hint is there: wool and cloth, the same perishable staples that started the English on the road to commercial empire. In-cidentally, the Russians maintain that the Mycenaeans imported their gold from Transylvania, which would give the two nations one more thing in common, the first being their frank admiration for the uses of toughness and guile to dominate others, an art of which Ulysses was a past master in every sense.

Almost synonymous with wine is the whole concept of hospitality, which is of primary importance to the Mycenaeans, for as we know, strangers are sent by Zeus. Thus, a noble guest is received without ques-tion, bathed, anointed, and dressed. His name and business are only in-quired about after the squires have blended mellow wine in mixing bowls—a choice wine, like Nestor's, being one that remains in its jar at

Telemachos' Bath at Pylos

least ten years before the maids undo its cap and broach it. Various meats are served on platters and boards in lavish portions, the choicest being the sirloin, which is sometimes passed by the host to his guest. With the meats come bread and "dainties," and the wine is often accompanied by olives and onions. So important is this hospitality that it is an offense to assume that it may not be offered, as Nestor indicates when Telemachos and Athena seem ready to start back toward their ship from the beach at Pylos, and he asks them if they think they are at the house of some pauper.

Gifts are of course a part of hospitality, and Menelaos offers Telemachos "a beautiful cup, three horses, and a splendid chariot" if he will stay for twelve days. Chariots are an important item of Mycenaean wealth, and Telemachos goes from Pylos to Sparta in two days in Nestor's, spending the night in Pharae, modern Kalamata. There we of *Oh Papa* landed without permission on our way to Pylos, which caused no trouble, for Greece is what I call a "yes country," where one can create an irregular *fait accompli* and then talk one's way out of it, as Ulysses so often did. I will leave the reader to identify his own "no countries," for which he will surely not have far to seek.

I have tried to sketch here the world that emerges so poetically from Homer and so prosaically from the tablets: a world surrounded by the endless ocean; a feudal world in which gods and men form an inseparable hierarchy, in which the land is one with the sea over which men sail cautiously in well-found ships, leaving behind women who are subordinate but by no means tame, and where all are careful of manners while not too worried about morals, since justice is a contract between individuals with room to spare, and imagination enough to fill it.

THROUGH THE CURTAIN

Troy, Tenedos, and Ismaros *(Izmir and the Cyclades)*

Malea and the Lotus-eaters *(The Submerged Port of the Phileni)*

The Cyclops *(Mallorca)*

Aiolos and the Sight of Home *(Minorca)*

TROY, TENEDOS, AND ISMAROS
(Izmir and the Cyclades)

Once alone with his own squadron, having left both Nestor and Agamemnon, Ulysses tells his story:

The same wind as wafted me from Ilium brought me to Ismarus, the city of the Cicones. I sacked this place and destroyed the men who held it. Their wives and the rich plunder that we took from the town we divided so that no one, as far as I could help it, should go short of his proper share. And then I said we ought to be off and show a clean pair of heels. But my fools of men refused. There was plenty of wine, plenty of livestock; and they kept on drinking and butchering sheep and fatted cattle by the shore. Meanwhile the Cicones went and raised a cry for help among other Cicones, their up-country neighbours, who are both more numerous and better men, trained in fighting from the chariot and on foot as well, as the occasion requires. At dawn they were on us, thick as the leaves and flowers in their season, and it certainly looked as though Zeus meant the worst for my unhappy following and we were in for a very bad time. A pitched battle by the ships ensued, and volleys of bronze spears were interchanged. Right through the early morning and while the blessed light of day grew stronger we held our ground and kept their greater force at bay; but when the sun began to drop, towards the time when the ploughman unyokes his ox, the Cicones gained the upper hand and broke the Achaean ranks. Six of my warriors from each ship were killed. The rest of us contrived to dodge our fate and got away alive.

We made off from Ismarus with heavy hearts, for the joy we felt at our own reprieve was tempered by grief for our dear comrades-in-arms; and I would not let the curved ships sail before each of our poor friends who had fallen in action against the Cicones had been three times saluted. Zeus, who marshals the clouds, now sent by fleet a terrible gale from the north. He covered land and sea alike with a canopy of cloud; and darkness swept down on us from the sky. Our ships were driven sidelong by the wind, and the force of the gusts tore their sails to rags and tatters. With the fear of death upon us we lowered these onto the decks, and rowed the bare ships landward with all our might. Thus we lay for two days and two nights on end, with exhaustion and anxiety gnawing at our hearts. But on the third morning, which a beautiful dawn had ushered in, we stepped the masts, hauled up the white sails, and sat down, leaving the wind and the helmsmen between them to keep our vessels straight.[1]

Hardly has Ulysses left Troy, when his words begin to lead us away from his traditional route, which calls for him to sail northwest from Troy to Thrace, there to sack the city of the Kikones. I propose that he sail south toward Lesbos like Nestor, then round the inland coast of that island, and into Chios Strait, on the mainland side of which and near its mouth (perhaps at Phocasa) I propose to place Ismaros, the city of the Kikones.[1] As our journey progresses, I hope to show that I am a good conservative who respects tradition whenever possible, but this first departure from tradition will serve well to pinpoint the kind of reasons that will lead me to my airborne conclusions, while other reasons led other men, as good or better but earthbound, to other conclusions that seemed reasonable from their point of view.

The location of Troy I will not discuss here, for Schliemann's archaeological confirmation of its traditional place has left few doubts. There is still some discussion as to which of the superimposed ruins (ranging from 3000 B.C. to A.D. 400) was Priam's, since Dörpfeld's Troy VI now appears to have been destroyed by an earthquake, while Blegen's Troy VII A (1300–1250 B.C.) looks more like the victim of siege and fire. But this does not concern us too much now; the important thing is that Ulysses must start for home from below the hill of Hissarlik, close to the southernmost corner of the Hellespont.

We know from Nestor that a northerly wind prevailed when he left Troy, enabling him to sail swiftly thence to Tenedos, Lesbos, and Gerais-

1. See chart page 33.

tos. Ulysses, who accompanied him as far as Tenedos, surely guessed his plan, which was based on signs from heaven read by the one Mycenaean king with whom Ulysses seldom if ever disagreed; why then did he leave the combined fleet and row back to Agamemnon's camp before Troy? For three reasons, and Nestor tells us the first: because, typically, Ulysses decided it would be wise, after having shown his independence, to get back on the side of the commander-in-chief. The second reason I propose: because, much as he trusted Nestor and his signs, he still preferred the easier and more profitable route along the straits of Lesbos and Chios, and through the Cyclades. And the third reason also: to Nestor, responsible commander of an important fleet whose home base was sandy Pylos, one of the great natural harbors of the Mediterranean, it was well worth risking the lonely hundred-mile passage diagonally across the Aegean, in order to put plenty of water between his fleet and the coast of Asia Minor, home of the allies of ruined Troy. But to pugnacious Ulysses it was obviously better not only to sail along a safer passage, but also to take the opportunity of sacking one more Asian city before returning home. As the rest of *The Odyssey* will show, he was never one to avoid confrontation with humans or even with monsters, whereas his experiences with the elements were usually more sobering. Whenever one sees his eyes light up at the joyous prospect of outwitting one more enemy, one is tempted to question his oft-lamented urgency to get home. Nevertheless, we must work on the assumption that he certainly would not purposely have sailed away from home without good reason. So why sail north from Troy to Thrace in the teeth of a north wind?

Ulysses himself confirms the presence of Nestor's north wind when he specifies that the same wind that brought him from Troy (to Tenedos) also brought him to Ismaros; that could hardly have been the south wind he would have needed to sail for Thrace. Then why did our predecessors ignore this north wind? Because their reasoning was traditional, mythological, or etymological rather than navigational. In this instance, they were attracted by Maronia in Thrace, because of Maron, the high priest of the Kikones, whom Ulysses spared and from whom he received the wine that would later save him from the Cyclops; and also by the fact that Herodotos speaks of Kikones in Thrace at the time of Xerxes. They also naturally tended to treat the adventures of the several homebound fleets as separate incidents, while my bird's-eye view is different because I have crisscrossed the Aegean repeatedly, each time in a matter of hours, and talked (for my own safety) with the meteorologists whose job it is to put together almost simultaneous information from the entire sea. Therefore, I feel confident in proposing what may have happened to several fleets in different parts of the Aegean when the famous *meltemi* began to blow "out of Thrace" (and therefore not toward it), as it did on the funeral pyre of Patroklos at the close of *The Iliad*. And as for Herodotos' Thracian Kikones, to me they are simply one more example of the Greek custom of carrying place names along the routes of colonization, of which we will note many instances as we sail with Ulysses.

There are other good reasons for placing Ismaros in the vicinity of the Gulf of Smyrna, modern Izmir, instead of in Thrace. First of all, if one is not in Nestor's hurry to get away from Asia, there are only two sensible ways to sail from Troy and Tenedos to mainland Greece and the Peloponnese without losing sight of land: one via Limnos, Ayios Eustratios, and the northern Sporades, and then through the Gulf of Euboia; and the other, via the straits of Lesbos and Chios, and through the Cyclades.[2] Both these routes are preferred even by modern yachtsmen, for neither includes what Nestor called a long or lonely passage; and the loneliness of a passage, to a seaman without a compass, comes more from the absence of a landmark toward which to steer than from the duration of the passage itself. In the Aegean islands there are few mountains higher than two thousand feet, so that any passage of more than sixty-five nautical miles is lonely, except the final one toward the mainland coast where there are much loftier mountains. But of the two safe ways home, only the second is practical with a strong north wind.

2. See chart page 33.

That is why I feel justified in proposing it as Ulysses' choice, for in this reconstruction of his Odyssey I will use a sailor's choice much as an archaeologist uses the taste of a whole generation of artists in placing and dating a piece of pottery. In fact, my job might be called "airborne archaeology."

There are also a number of interesting coincidences to support my Asian Kikones: the fact that when the inland Kikones came to the rescue of their coastal cousins they fought from chariots, which was characteristic, if not exclusively, of the legendary warriors of Asia Minor; the similarity between the names of Smyrna (Izmir) and Ismaros; and the fact that the historical gap between *The Iliad* and *The Odyssey*—that is, between the siege of Troy and the voyage home—was filled by Quintus of Smyrna (see Bibliography), who may have been heir to a tradition left by Ulysses at his first stop on the way home from Troy.

Finally there is Ulysses' description of the sudden gale from the north, which drove his fleet "sidelong" until it was forced to seek the shore. If Ulysses had been sailing home from Thrace, the north wind would have been a following wind, and Ulysses would not have been driven sidelong by the gale, nor would he have been able to row ashore in its teeth. But after he had sailed south through the Straits of Chios, I suggest that the gale caught him near the western tip of Samos, sailing west toward Ikaria, the land of his maternal grandfather and a sensible place to seek refuge. The *Sailing Directions for the Mediterranean* even indicate where: "The coast southward of Beacon Hill on the southeastern side of Ikaria Island is a curved sandy beach, affording shelter from northerly and northwesterly winds."[3] And note that Boreas, Homer's north wind, is still called *bora* in the Adriatic, and a sudden gale is called *borrasca* in Spanish.

Now my weather map[4] shows that the *meltemi* is produced by a low pressure system over the Middle East, and a high pressure system over

3. U.S.H.O. 56, 8–172.
4. See chart page 56, courtesy of N. Klissiotis.

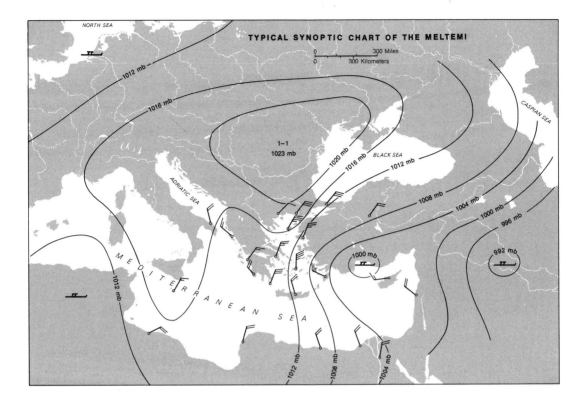

56

the Balkans, for in the Northern Hemisphere the winds flow clockwise around a high and counterclockwise around a low, just as when a bathtub empties the water forms a vortex around the drain. The sailing directions tell us that the winds out of the north are most persistent in the southeast Aegean Sea, where they reach the exceptional frequency of 80 percent or more in July and August. In summer the sky is seldom overcast and is often cloudless for days at a time, but in winter the southeastern Aegean, especially Samos, has the greatest rainfall, and before northerly gales the mountains are shrouded by dense cloud masses. Under such circumstances the currents in the straits set generally southward, and the lee or southern side of the islands is much safer for shipping.[5]

All this not only agrees with Ulysses' own detailed observations as quoted, but also with what was pointed out in Chapter I: that Boreas usually brings good weather in summer and bad in winter. Therefore, the episode probably occurred in fall, perhaps in September, the expeditionaries having left Troy in the hope that the summer weather would hold, and having been caught by an early sample of the coming winter.

So I propose my itinerary for the return of the four fleets from Troy,[6] and it shows that my relocation of Ismaros allows me to blame the same quite extraordinary storm for forcing the bulk of Menelaos' fleet into Crete, the red-haired King himself with his flag squadron all the way to Egypt, and Ulysses with his flotilla into the Gulf of Sirte, all of which makes navigational sense if one refers again to the weather chart. There we note how one and the same *meltemi* parts over Crete, under the south coast of which strong opposing eddies must be formed if the theory of aerodynamics is to be respected, then blows out of the northwest toward Egypt, and out of the northeast toward Cyrenaica. This, I think, clears up an episode that has hitherto remained confused, and also shows how Diomedes pulled into Argos (modern Nauplia, over which the fort-

5. U.S.H.O. 56, 1–36, 1–39, 1–44, 1–45, 1–54.
6. See chart page 59.

ress at Tiryns still watches) and Nestor pressed on to Pylos, just in time to escape the fate of Menelaos and Ulysses at Malea. In fact, once satisfied that the Great Storm was one and the same for all, one could even abandon meteorology altogether and contemplate the possibility that this was not an ordinary storm at all but a *tsunami* or *maremoto*, caused by some great volcanic eruption such as the one that destroyed Thira, today's Santorin. But that must await more investigation by men like Leon Pomerance, who has interpreted geological evidence to show that Thira erupted three times, the third close to 1200 B.C. and therefore to the fall of Troy.[7]

The flights of *Oh Papa* over the eastern Aegean will be described in Chapter IV, when we finally head for Cyprus, so here let me proceed directly to list in order of importance the criteria that have guided me in my first proposal, criteria that I will continue to develop and to use through the rest of our search:

1. *Navigation and meteorology.* The *meltemi* out of the north, the possible routes home from Troy, the Great Storm, and, given all these, the basic question, "What would a sailor have done?"

2. *Geographic descriptions.* Those that led Schliemann to Troy, navigational "anchor" of this first leg of Ulysses' voyage.

3. *Archaeology.* Again Schliemann's Troy and also Blegen's Pylos, leaving the reader to search for ancient Ismaros somewhere near the mouth of the Gulf of Izmir.

4. *Character.* Ulysses' wily wavering between his different allies, and his marked preference for fighting against men rather than against the elements.

5. *Names.* Ismaros-Smyrna-Izmir, though too much must not be made of this kind of coincidence, for, as has been pointed out, ancient Greek names traveled as well as Maron's wine.

7. James C. Loeb Classical Lecture, Harvard, April 15, 1969. Just such a *tsunami* appears in the legend of the death of Theseus' son, well described by Mary Renault (see Bibliography).

ITINERARY FROM TROY

	NESTOR	DIOMEDES	MENELAOS	ULYSSES
1st day 1st night	Troy-Tenedos-Lesbos Sacrifice	Troy-Tenedos-Lesbos Sacrifice	Troy-Tenedos-Lesbos Sacrifice	Troy-Tenedos Tenedos-Troy
2nd day 2nd night	Sacrifice Lesbos-Geraistos	Sacrifice Lesbos-Geraistos	Sacrifice Lesbos-Geraistos	Troy-Ismaros Sack and feast
3rd day 3rd night	Sacrifice Sacrifice	Sacrifice Sacrifice	Sacrifice Sacrifice	Fight inland: Kikones Sail (to escape) then Meltemi
4th day 4th night	Geraistos-Malea Sleep ashore	Geraistos-Argos (Meltemi not yet at Malea)	Geraistos-Sounion (Death of Phrontis)	Storm Sheltered in the lee Storm of Ikaria
5th day 5th night	Malea-Pylos (Meltemi not yet at Malea)		Burial Burial	Storm Sheltered in the lee Storm of Ikaria
6th day 6th night			Sounion-Malea Malea-Phaestus-Egypt (Meltimi)	Malea (temporary bonanza) Malea-Libya (Meltimi)

6. *Legends.* The legendary fighting chariots of Asia, though legends, like names, must be used with care since they often grew out of Homer in the first place, and should therefore not be used to support him as an historian.

MALEA AND THE LOTUS-EATERS
(*The Submerged Port of the Phileni*)

In fact I should have reached my own land safe and sound, had not the swell, the current, and the North Wind combined, as I was doubling Malea, to drive me off my course and send me drifting past Cythera.

For nine days I was chased by those accursed winds across the fish-infested seas. But on the tenth we made the country of the Lotus-eaters, a race that live on vegetable foods. We disembarked to draw water, and my crews quickly set to on their midday meal by the ships. But as soon as we had a mouthful and a drink, I sent some of my followers inland to find out what sort of human beings might be there, detailing two men for the duty with a third as messenger. Off they went, and it was not long before they were in touch with the Lotus-eaters. Now it never entered the heads of these natives to kill my friends; what they did was to give them some lotus to taste, and as soon as each had eaten the honeyed fruit of the plant, all thoughts of reporting to us or escaping were banished from his mind. All they now wished for was to stay where they were with the Lotus-eaters, to browse on the lotus, and to forget that they had a home to return to. I had to use force to bring them back to the ships, and they wept on the way, but once on board I dragged them under the benches and left them in irons.[ii]

So does Ulysses leave the known world at Malea, trailing in his wake the imagination of more than a hundred generations. Lita's photograph[8] shows Cape Malea from the southwest, as the helpless Ulysses must have seen it before it disappeared below the northeastern horizon; and Lita has caught a ship ready to round it as Ulysses must have done on his way to Troy.

8. See photo page 61.

Cape Malea

We flew over Malea on our way to Ithaka and Corfu from Athens. At the hotel in Athens, we had overheard an American father, sitting in his room with the door open, reading excerpts from Mr. Hilton's official prose to his openmouthed family, which reminded me that chasing Ulysses in an airplane is probably the least of my eccentricities in this modern world. This impression was confirmed on the day of our departure when we rose early and prepared for a quick takeoff, which was prevented by the hour-long queue of "tours" waiting to sign their bills at the cashier's. Anachronistically traveling around on my own without reservations, I waited to pay in cash, of all things, and was struck by the contemporary ring of the cashier's lament when her IBM failed to live up to the situation: "These guests, they create such problems for my machines. . . ." Once at the airport, I again made the mistake of trying to dispatch things simply. The official who received my flight plan could not conceive of flying from Athens to Corfu along any path different from the high and straight airways that are standard for commercial airline flights, at least not for licit purposes. Had it not been for the arrival of pilots Teophilis and Papanastasiou, who came to see us off, I would have been forced to lie about my plans, a solution not too dangerous since one can be sure that there are no other aircraft with flight plans for the low altitudes I fly at in order to make my observations and take our pictures. Our friends not only solved all our problems in a most military way, but they also offered us an excellent lunch at the airport restaurant, during which Carlos Aristimuño, who accompanied us aloft on this part of our flight, spotted two Orthodox priests appraising a small aircraft they were planning to buy for transportation to and from the monastery at Mount Athos, where to this day no female, human or animal, is permitted. The Greek word for "light plane" cannot be feminine in gender as it is in Spanish (*avioneta*).

During our stay in the capital I was able to discuss my theories with Spyridon Marinatos, Director of Archaeology of Greece, whose work is known to all interested in the Mycenaean world. I visited him first at his office, and then Lita and I dined with him and his wife and some of his colleagues at his home. Far from distrusting my unorthodox approach to *The Odyssey*, Marinatos was amused by it, and encouraged me in my purpose. Thanks to my position as president of the International Aviation Federation, of which King Constantine, a keen pilot, is a patron, I was also taken by the president of the Aeroclub of Greece to the summer palace at Tatoi to visit the King, who had read *The Caribbean as Columbus Saw It* and was therefore familiar with my aerial view of history. He also encouraged me to follow Ulysses as Morison and I had followed Columbus, and asked me to send him my conclusions, which I certainly plan to do, though he is now far from his country.

But to return to Ulysses and his transit out of the known world, his own words leave little doubt that it was a renewed *meltemi* that blew him away from Malea, so that here I thought I need not stray too far from tradition, and could look for his next landfall somewhere in the Libyan Gulf of Sirte, since most nineteenth-century maps of the Ancient World place the land of the Lotus-eaters on the island of Djerba, ancient Minix, or somewhere near it. In this case, of the criteria mentioned before, the dominant ones must be navigation and meteorology, since Homer's text gives no description of the place. As to the time taken to reach it, we have our first example of the magic numbers, in this case 9; but even if we wished to take it literally, our calculated speed of two knots for a ship being blown unwillingly during nine days and nights could put Ulysses almost anywhere inside the Gulf of Sirte.

Nevertheless, before accepting Djerba, I decided to check the first atlas of all, and was fortunate in obtaining for my library the facsimile edition [9] of the *Cosmographia* of Claudius Ptolomaeus, printed in Bologna in 1477 with maps engraved by Taddeo Crivelli. This atlas, the first to add maps to Ptolemy's classic text, handed down, with improvements, since about A.D. 150, correctly places Troy, and as will be seen in my

9. See Bibliography.

reproduction of the appropriate part of Crivelli's map,[10] the "*Lattopagi*" (i.e., Lotophagi or Lotus-eaters) are here situated not near the island of Djerba (Minix) as in later maps, but toward the bottom of the Gulf of Syrtis Major, not far from a city identified as Phileni Villa, which sits at the southernmost point of the whole Mediterranean. In the next edition of Ptolemy (1482), which I checked in Holland, I also found Phileni Villa, as well as one more example of the fact that ancient names are nomads, for both Russian Georgia and Albania are here labeled "Iberia." This reminded me of a visit to Tiflis, where, over too much white wine, our Russian friends failed to make Lita understand Georgian, although they claimed it was related to Basque. In this edition of Ptolemy, Ilium, Tenedos, Pylos, Ithaka, and Cabrera are all correctly identified, Skylla and Charybdis are at Messina, "Mago" on Minorca, and near Bonifacio is a legendary "Titani Port," the Port of the Giants. Both the 1477 and 1488 Ptolemys omit Cape Circeo. All these facts will be useful to us later.

I decided to fly low the length of the Libyan gulf, from Tripoli to Bengazi, a distance of almost three hundred nautical miles, which, I was warned, was all desert. We spent the night at Tripoli, a city surrounded by olive groves coaxed from the desert, and boasting a *passeggiata*, both tributes to Italian colonization, though we found Tripoli overrun by German and American oilmen, soon, probably, to be replaced by Russians. Next day we flew over the magnificent ruins of Roman Leptis Magna, and headed southeast along the Libyan coast, our left wing skimming a sea of pure turquoise, while our right almost raised the dust off an endless desert of varying shades of ocher, peopled only by very occasional tribes of nomads who watched us pass with evident surprise. For hours we saw nothing of interest, until patience as well as gasoline were beginning to run down, for low flight is notoriously gas-consuming, and I was beginning to agree with the friends who had counseled against this part of the expedition. Then, at the bottom of the gulf, and just as I was

10. See chart page 65.

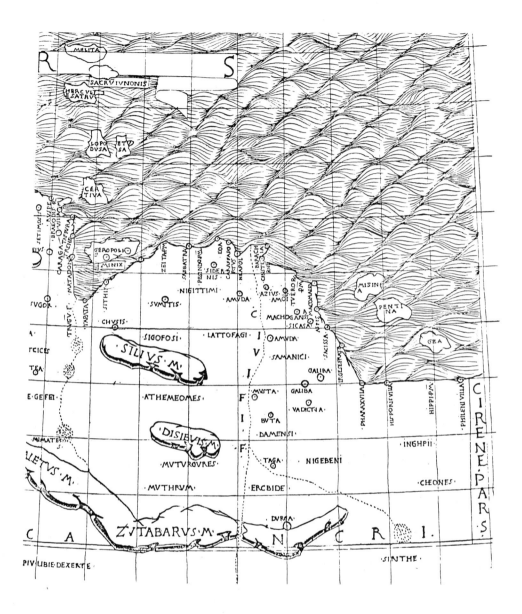

R S

MELITA

SACRV IVNONIS

HERCVLT E SATRV

LOPO DVSA   ET SA

CERTIVA

ELVS ETIMOTO   BRAEOLI   THAPVRA

CALAGA   MATADOL   ALENE

GEROPOLIO

MINIX

ELVS

SITHI

ZEITAPA   SABBATRA   PEDNO EOA   EOA   CANAPARO   RETVS   NEAPOL   BARACH   CONTOFALA   RVE

AZIVS AMOI

NIGITTIMI   AMVDA   TVERORV

MISINA

FVGOR   TNGV.   TABATA   CHVSIS   SVMVTIS   MACHOGANSS   SICASA   PENTINA

AREICES   TEA   SIGOFOSI   LATTOFAGI   C   AMVDA   I   SACISSA   GEA

SILIVS·M·   SAMANICI   V   GALIBA   LEGEDERTA

E·GEFEI   ATHEMEOMES·   F   MVSTA   GALIBA   PHINAXVILA   HIPPOSINA   HIPPIFIV   PHILENI VILLA   CIRENE·PARS

I   VADICTA

MIMATES   S.   DISIEVISM·   BVTA   DAMENSI   INGHPII

UETVS·M·   MVTVROVRES·   F   TAGA·   NIGEBENI   CHEONES

MVTHRVM·   ERCBIDE

 C   A   ZVTABARVS·M·   DVRAA   N   C   R   I·

PIVUBIE·DEXERTE   SINTHE·

65

ready to climb and set a direct course for Bengazi, we saw jutting out from the coast a high rock crowned with the unmistakable remains of something constructed by human hands. And at the foot of the rock, clearly visible from the air, we saw the shape of a small submerged port. We circled excitedly, and Lita snapped away, ducking to keep out of the way of the laundry she had hung up to dry in the back of the plane, so hopeless had she considered this part of the trip. This domestic scene in our airplane is not surprising: she sometimes even crochets in the co-pilot's seat, which really puts me off. Since she steadfastly refuses to learn to pilot my plane, if I fail in midair she will have to weave her way out of the problem, like Penelope.

Her photo [11] shows the port of the Phileni as we located it from the air, and though it is identified in our Ptolemy, as well as in some modern atlases of the Ancient World, we have been unable to learn more about the place: no one seems to have studied these ruins, and no one has been able to tell us who the Phileni were, or why they should have built altars (*arae*, as the nineteenth-century historical atlases have it) or a city (*villa*, as Ptolemy has it), at the southernmost point in the entire Mediterranean Sea. But it does fall just about where I would expect to find the Lotophagi if I had been blown to their land from Malea by the *meltemi*—either missing Bengazi in the storm or being unable to row across such a powerful gale—somewhat to the east of Djerba where they have usually been placed, but not too far east of the site marked on the very first atlas. Most importantly, it lies on the borders of the kingdom of Put, close to Egypt, where Helen got her magic potions, not unlike those that nearly induced two of Ulysses' sailors to stay (which I am sure they later wished a thousand times they had done). Incidentally, Ptolemy also has an inland Philae near the cataracts of the Nile, which is one more example of the migration of names. Another was my last "checkpoint" before the port of the Phileni, an abandoned British

11. See photo page 67.

The Submerged Port of the Lotus-eaters, Arae Philenorum

67

airport of the Second World War, still known as "Marble Arch," which may puzzle future generations, much as we have to think twice to remember that Columbus called the island San Juan, and the port Puerto Rico, names which have since, illogically, changed places.

When I got back to my library, I found another quite extraordinary witness for my Philenian Lotophagi: our friend Scylax of Caryanda, who in my first chapter helped me estimate the speed of Ulysses' ship, and who, according to Herodotos, sailed for Darius I. His *Periplus*, according to modern criticism, contains information from the sixth, fifth, and principally, the fourth century B.C., though the oldest Codex, preserved at the Bibliothèque Nationale in Paris, only dates from the twelfth century A.D. He describes the gulf of Libya thus: "After the Hesperides is a large bay, by name Syrtis, which may be put at 5000 stadia at least. Its width from Hesperides to Neapolis, which lies on the opposite shore, is a three days and nights sail. Round this there lives a Libyan people, the Nasamones, down to the inmost corner on the left. . . . In the inmost creek of the Syrtis are the altars of Philaenus, a wharf, and a grove of Ammon of Syrtis. . . . The parts beyond the Syrtis are inhabited by a Libyan people, the Lotophagi, as far as the mouth of the Syrtis. These use the Lotus for food and drink." [12] So, reader, if you are in the neighborhood, try to identify the port of the Phileni with that of the philandering Lotophagi, for on that faceless coast, what other port could Ulysses have chosen? As to the lotus itself, all sorts of suggestions have been made, but I incline toward *Lotus pulcherimus*, in Spanish *martillo*, an aphrodisiac nut.

Oh Papa did not have enough gas to tarry long over our find, though I did clearly hear the ancient voice of the Lotophagi inciting me to attempt a landing on the desert and take a look at their submerged port,

12. Quoted by Nordenskiöld (see Bibliography). "The inmost corner on the left" can well be the bottom of the gulf as seen from the Mediterranean, for the practice of placing the north at the top of a map is quite modern. The basin of the Sirte, now rich in oil, is about a hundred miles south of our sunken port.

which I imagined surrounded by the verdure that then covered today's Libyan desert. But I resisted (or I might still be there), and, rejoicing in the thought that our scorching desert flight had not been useless, I climbed into the cooler air above, leaned my engines to a more comfortable mixture, and headed for Bengazi. There I landed with just enough daylight left to try to make Athens. I decided to taxi to a spot directly under the control tower, where I could hope to tank up, get a weather forecast for the water-hop to Greece, file a new flight plan, and be off without so much as a "by your leave" to the customs, who would certainly have made an all-night production out of this strictly technical stop. Lita stayed in the plane while I climbed the usual flights of stairs, got a favorable forecast from a Chinese meteorologist, and filed my flight plan with a British official who gave me two useful pieces of advice. First, he agreed that I was well advised not to go near the customs if I was not planning to stay. "You never know with these fellows" he said, referring to his employer, the Sovereign Government of Libya. And second, he advised me to relieve myself off the roof on my way out of the control tower if I did not wish to walk all the way to the terminal building. But not, of course, to windward, he added, with the voice of experience.

This operation completed, I took off as quickly as possible and headed north toward the western tip of Crete and the Island of Kythera, the last familiar land Ulysses saw, which Lita managed to photograph in the failing light. Thence I proceeded to Athens amid a crescendo of chatter from jets in the darkening sky, all converging on Glyfada Airport, their vapor trails like road signs in the sky. My small voice in this chorus surprised everyone, for it is evidently not usual for a small plane to request a visual landing among the giants on "instrument flight rules" in the land where all men, except slaves and a few others, were first declared equal. But after a polylingual discussion and some dodging to keep out of the way of the heavy traffic, we landed, and cleared customs.

So we left behind the great Gulf of Sirte, where Ulysses clapped in irons the scouts he had sent ashore, who had so easily succumbed to the hallucination of the lotus that they never wished to see home or family again. He pushed them under the benches of his ships, and shoved off in haste, lest temptation beckon once more, an exit somewhat similar to ours, *mutatis mutandis.*

THE CYCLOPS
(Mallorca)

I then commanded the rest of my loyal band to embark with all speed on their fast ships, for fear that others of them might eat the lotus and think no more of home. They came on board at once, went to the benches, sat down in their proper places, and struck the white surf with their oars.

So we left that country and sailed on sick at heart. And we came to the land of the Cyclopes, a fierce, uncivilized people who never lift a hand to plant or plough but put their trust in Providence. All the crops they require spring up unsown and untilled, wheat and barley and the vines whose generous clusters give them wine when ripened for them by the timely rains. The Cyclopes have no assemblies for the making of laws, nor any settled customs, but live in hollow caverns in the mountain heights, where each man is law-giver to his children and his wives, and nobody cares a jot for his neighbours.

Not very far from the harbour on their coast, and not so near either, there lies a luxuriant island, covered with woods, which is the home of innumerable goats. . . . I must explain that the Cyclopes have nothing like our ships with their crimson prows. . . . Also it has a safe harbour, in which there is no occasion to tie up at all. . . . Finally, at the head of the harbour there is a stream of fresh water, running out of a cave in a grove of poplar-trees.

This is where we came to land. . . .

When the fresh Dawn came and with her crimson streamers lit the sky . . . we fetched our curved bows and our long spears from the ships, separated into three parties, and let fly at the game . . . and as we looked across at the neighbouring land of the Cyclopes, we could not only see the smoke from their fires but hear their voices and the bleating of their sheep and goats. . . .[iii]

We made out a cave there, close to the sea, with a high entrance overhung by laurels. Here large flocks of sheep and goats were penned at night.[iv]

Ulysses, at the head of his twelve ships, rows away from the land of the Lotus-eaters; and when a seaman in a small ship sets a course, there are three main questions that determine it: where is the wind, where is he himself, and where does he want to go? Of the wind, Homer tells us only that Ulysses' men had to row to get away from the tempting land of the lotus; and as to where Ulysses wanted to go, we have no reason to doubt that he wanted to go home; so the question remains: Where did he think he was?

The more common experience for those who were blown away from Malea by the *meltemi* was to fetch up in Egypt, as did Menelaos, so that for the next leg of our Odyssey it is reasonable to suppose that Ulysses thought he was in Egypt, though even through the darkness of the storm that drove him, he probably had sufficient glimpses of the sun's light to realize that he was somewhat to the west of the Nile delta. So, once again, we come to the question: What will a sailor do? If he thinks he is in western Egypt, and his objective is the Peloponnese, the answer is clear: he must sail or row along the coast as long as it tends toward the northwest, and when it begins to turn to the southwest he will know that he has reached its northernmost point. Then he will wait for favorable conditions, say his prayers, sail north, and expect to see the great mountains of the Peloponnese (or perhaps of Crete), which on a clear day are visible from well over one hundred nautical miles away, that is to say for about two-thirds of the crossing.

But Ulysses has traditionally been supposed to have sailed directly north from the land of the Lotus-eaters, and since this was usually placed at Djerba, it was deduced that he would sail into the Tyrrhenian Sea, with or without a stop in Sicily, where many placed the Cyclops, some even identifying the monster's eye with that of the volcano Etna. With this I cannot agree. No seaman, or airman for that matter, will set a course across open water from an unknown coast, just as no golfer will try to drive a ball over the woods toward a hidden green without knowing the position of his tee relative to that green. And least of all would wily Ulysses have attempted this senseless feat of navigation when it meant embarking upon the very type of lonely ocean crossing that even Nestor preferred to make only for a very good reason.

So here I have no hesitation in staying away from tradition and proposing that Ulysses first led his fleet along the Libyan coast to the northwest and continued on that course until, after crossing the Gulf of Carthage, he reached present-day Bizerte at the northern tip of Tunisia, where the coast takes a definite turn to the southwest, and was therefore no longer worth following. Then and only then did Ulysses await favorable conditions, offer the proper sacrifices, and set sail toward the north, his eyes soon scouring the horizon for the mountains of the Peloponnese.

Now it is well known that in the straits separating Sardinia from Tunisia, the *sirocco* (southeaster) alternates with the *tramontana* (northeaster), and between them those two great winds dominate this stretch of sea. Consequently my supposition is that, though Ulysses probably set sail from Tunis with a favorable wind out of the south, before he got very far the wind veered to the northeast, and he was forced to lower his sail and row, unwilling to abandon his northerly course for home. And if so, it is not unreasonable to suppose that he was blown progressively off course toward the west, where an island awaited him that to this day is called Cabrera, Spanish for "island of the goats," strikingly similar to the one he describes as his next landfall. And our *Sailing Directions for the Mediterranean* state repeatedly that an east wind prevails along the coast of North Africa, sometimes lasting a week in summer and in fall, which would suit my idea that Ulysses left Troy in September.[13]

But before accepting this hypothesis, let us for a moment consider the

13. U.S.H.O. 52, 53.

alternatives: Suppose Ulysses was not blown off course but, on the contrary, succeeded in sailing north from Tunisia or even from Djerba, what then? Then it would have taken him no time at all to spot the mountains of Sardinia and to realize his mistake, for there is little similarity between Sardinia and the Peloponnese or Crete as seen from the south. And the distance from Tunisia to Sardinia is about half that from Libya to Greece, so that at this early stage he would most probably have turned back, rather than press on into another unknown land. Nevertheless, it is possible to conjecture Ulysses' landing in Sardinia, as others have brought him to the western tip of Sicily, but this brings up the greatest difficulty of all traditional itineraries. Whether from southern Sardinia or from western Sicily, and knowing as he must by then that he has not sailed from Libya to the Peloponnese, why would Ulysses insist on sailing far into the north, which he would have to do in order to reach Bonifacio at the southern tip of Corsica, a landfall about which few commentators entertain any doubts? Not only is there no reason for him to have sailed far to the north, but as my quotation under "Aiolos and the Sight of Home" (page 83) will clearly show, he actually reached Bonifacio with a west wind, so that at this stage it is indispensable to get him well to the west of the Tyrrhenian.

And there are many other good reasons for proposing that a change of wind must have brought Ulysses to the Balearics, too far to think of turning back (a thought that does not seem to have crossed his mind) and far enough to the west for the rest of his course to make sense. Our photograph [14] shows that Cabrera and its port correspond perfectly with Ulysses' description. And across the narrow water stand the mountains of Mallorca, riddled with prehistoric caves, from which the smoke could easily have announced the fires of the Cyclopes who, like my Spanish ancestors from the beginning of time, "preferred never to lift a hand to plant or plow but put their trust in Providence . . . each a lawgiver to his

14. See photo page 74.

Goat Island, Cabrera

74

children and his wives, nobody caring a jot for his neighbors."

To investigate the Balearics, Lita and I flew from Barcelona, where we had arrived after waiting three days in Paris for the tail end of a European hurricane to disappear, though we thought we had left such problems behind in the Caribbean. Even when the weather cleared, our takeoff was unhurried. The Citroën that was to take us to where *Oh Papa* waited in front of customs would not start, so we had to push it, and at customs we spent some more time helping a happy English group that had just landed from London in a plane even smaller than ours, which probably explains why they did not bring a French dictionary.

Once in Barcelona, after filing our flight plan, we were warned by a solemn colonel that there was such a great deal of traffic over Mallorca that his island counterpart might well send us back to Barcelona, and that "consequently" it was compulsory to fly low over the water. We said yes, yes, shoved our luggage in a pushcart to *Oh Papa* (no Citroën here), and took off. Then we flew high over the water, as prudence dictates on a perfectly clear day in which we saw no traffic at all, and low around the island, after contacting the control tower, which gave us no trouble at all. Even in Spain there are colonels and colonels.

Mallorca's beautiful northwest coast stands vertically out of the water like a family of huge sea monsters who have come up for air and may at any moment plunge back into the depths. The southeast coast, on the other hand, once beyond dramatic Andraitx, bows down into a fertile plain that pays court to the great bay of Palma, generously tranquil in the sea. This plain could well have provided the Cyclopes with "all the crops they required, unsown and untilled"; but what interested me most was the extreme south point of the island, a few miles off which lies the island of Cabrera, with its small, safe port. And as we flew low over Cabrera to take our pictures, we could see in the distance the mountains of Mallorca, from which the smoke of the Cyclopes seemed to rise, and the abrupt southeast coast, which we knew to be famous for its great caves, as is barren Minorca, a short hop across the straits along the same line of sight.

Flying low toward Formentor on the northeast corner of Mallorca, we completed our circuit of the island, and spotted several of the caves, such as those of *El Drach* (The Dragon). At Formentor we rested a few days at the beautiful hotel, and we explored another cave at the top of a mountain to which we were taken by a shepherd named Perico, who claimed to have found copper implements there, and promised that it was only a few minutes walk up the hill. We spent the whole afternoon getting there, and ended up climbing on all fours, which is the proper position for a neophyte archaeologist. The monstrous cave, with its beautiful view of the sea, was nevertheless worth the climb, and, though we found no implements, we did dig up some bones that could have been those of the men Polyphemos devoured before Ulysses blinded him with the stake he heated at the great fire, of which we were also reminded by traces of charcoal and ashes. I mention this to show the reader that if he agrees on Cabrera as Ulysses' landfall, he has a good choice of caves for Polyphemos, not only on Mallorca but also on nearby Minorca, which archaeologically belongs to the same group.

To fly low around Minorca, as we did next, is to use one's aircraft to return to the Stone Age. Framed by a beautiful coast full of *calas* (small bays) and deep fjords such as those that form its two principal ports, Mahón and Ciudadela, this island is a great stone table studded with hundreds of stone monuments, conical, in the form of monumental T's or tables, or shaped like upturned boats, which from the air make it look like the world's richest archaeological park. Once one is on the ground, many of these monuments prove to be the modern *gairitas* in which the local peasants, following the architecture of their forgotten forefathers, try to accumulate the rocks that litter their fields and seem to spring up faster than they are removed. But this still leaves hundreds of prehistoric *talayots* ("towers" in Catalan), *taulas* ("tables") and *navetas* ("ships"), in clusters that include great caves whose roofs are often propped up with enormous monoliths, and are sometimes interconnected by tunnels.

On landing, we had to leave all our papers at the airport as we had at Mallorca, but here the strange custom was explained. Not long before our visit, Mr. Tshombe, the rebel premier of Katanga in the Congo, had been lured onto a private airplane while vacationing in the Balearics, and had been flown to African captivity, where he died. So the tourist-conscious authorities had decided to take precautions so that the islands would not regain their ancient reputation by receiving visitors in a way reminiscent of Ulysses' reception by the Cyclops. But unlike the airport at Mallorca, which looks like a Scandinavian colony, on Minorca there is no ballyhoo for tourists, and we even had a hard time arranging to rent a Seat-600, a car the size of a wheelbarrow that performs like a jeep, as we soon found out on the island's "neolithic" roads.

Once organized, we were lucky indeed in finding María Luisa Serra, the island's Director of Archaeology, to whom we had an introduction from Francisco Martí of the Archaeological Museum of Barcelona. She was working late in her museum, which stands on top of a hive of pre-historic cave dwellings and contains abundant exhibits of Stone Age relics, as well as "Mycenaean" stone hinges, "Cycladic" jugs, and bronze implements (more of which are in the private collection of Pons y Soler), suggesting that neolithic conditions survived in these parts well into the Bronze Age. In other words, Ulysses could have sailed from luxurious Troy to the barbarous land of Polyphemos without one's need-ing to describe as legendary his trip through time as well as through space.

In the museum, and later at our hotel, Miss Serra introduced us to the surprisingly sparse archaeological literature concerning this island, and to the traditions that connect its capital, Mahón (Magon), with the giant Mago (Gog and Magog), and, according to Titus Livius, made the Minorcans in Roman times famous as slingers of stones after Hannibal proved their worth. This specialty, so reminiscent of giant Polyphemos' attempt to sink Ulysses' ship with rocks, the Minorcans

Polyphemos' Cave - Menorca

78

still learn as children, slinging stones to round up their cattle. Strabo, the Augustan historian, says they used to learn it by throwing stones at the food their mothers placed out of reach. In any case, their skill soon made them the object of both Carthaginian and Roman "levies," and sent their stones to battle all over the Ancient World. Miss Serra also showed us how she had reconstructed the *Naveta del Tudons*, but assured us that neither its purpose nor that of any other monuments on the island has ever been explained. The government has generally left the monuments unexplored and unguarded, satisfied that it has done its job by passing a decree succinctly entitled "Instructions for the Defense of the Archaeological and Scientific Prehistoric and Protohistoric Monuments of the Island of Minorca, by the Artistic, Archaeological, and Ethnological Information Service." And Minorcan peasants seem to approve, for no sooner had Miss Serra placed a sign at the entrance of her reconstructed *naveta*, than someone shot it full of holes.

Lita and I set off to visit the monuments in our indestructible mini-jeep, which could just pass between the two high stone walls that frame most of the stone-strewn roads of this stoniest of islands. And imagine our happy surprise when the first cave we entered proved to be full of Polyphemos' sheep.[15] The shelter of caves, natural or made by ancient or modern man, has by no means been abandoned on this island, where the midday sun slings his rays as if they were yet more stones; and I even saw a motorcycle parked in one. As to the other monuments, I am attracted by Miss Serra's idea that the *taulas* [16] are the remains of props or columns for artificial caves like the ones we explored.[17] For the *navetas*,[18] I have my own suggestion: might not the Cyclopes, who according to Ulysses had no ships, have built the upturned "ships" as precautionary "ex-votos" against the return of the black ship that brought Ulysses, that

15. See photo page 78.
16. See photo page 80.
17. See photo page 82.
18. See photo page 85.

Minorcan *Taula*

dreadful dwarf whose cunning vanquished their giant king under their very noses?

Before takeoff from the Balearics I filled *Oh Papa*'s tanks to the top in order to explore from the air the whole of Spain's east coast, and then proceed to Africa; and this operation, which required one man to hold the funnel, another to pour the gas, and half a dozen to encourage them, reminded me again of the Cyclopes, who "never lifted a hand . . ."

As far as it has been studied, the archaeology of Mallorca, though much poorer in monuments, is similar to that of neighboring Minorca. So, though I have preferred to use Lita's photo of a Minorcan cave for the Cyclops, my proposal is that the Cyclopes' "mainland" was Mallorca, within sight of Cabrera, where Ulysses beached his ships after fleeing from the land of the Lotus-eaters. I think it was on Mallorca that he outwitted the Cyclops, who had trapped him and his men in his cave full of sheep, by giving the Cyclops the Kikones' wine unwatered, and making him drunk; whereupon he put the giant's eye out with the burning stake, tricked him into rolling back the door stone, and rode out hugging the fleecy belly of a ram—but not before the giant had devoured six of Ulysses' men. And as the wily Greek sailed away, still taunting his enemy with his great laugh, the blinded Cyclops hurled his last stones, perhaps the first thrown in war by a Balear, nearly sinking the black-prowed ship. This unfortunate Cyclops, Polyphemos, was the son of Poseidon, the sea god, who begat him in a cavern on Thöosa the Nymph, daughter of Phorkys, the Old Man of the Sea. And it is the hatred of Poseidon for Ulysses that is to hound the Ithakan to the very end of the Odyssey, just as Polyphemos requests: "Father, may Ulysses, sacker of Cities, never get to his home in Ithaka. But if he must, let him arrive late, in evil plight, and all his comrades dead. And when he is landed by a foreign ship, let him find trouble in his home." ▾

Minorcan Cave Dwelling

AIOLOS AND THE SIGHT OF HOME
(Minorca)

Climbing in at once, they went to the benches, sorted themselves out, and struck the grey water with their oars. Thus we left the island. . . .

Our next landfall was the floating island of Aeolia, the home of Aeolus son of Hippotas, who is a favourite of the immortal gods. All round this isle there runs an unbroken wall of bronze, and below it the cliffs rise sheer from the sea. . . .

For a whole month Aeolus was my kind host. . . . I asked him whether I might now continue my journey and count on his help. He gave it willingly and presented me with a leather bag, made from the flayed skin of a full-grown ox, in which he had imprisoned the boisterous energies of all the Winds. For you must know that Zeus has made him Warden of the Gales, with power to lay or rouse them each at will. This pouch he stowed in the hold of my ship, securing it tightly with a burnished silver wire so as to prevent the slightest leakage. Then, for my present purpose, he called up a breeze from the west to blow my ships and their crews across the sea. . . .

For the next nine days we sailed on, day and night; and on the tenth we were already in sight of our homeland, and had actually come near enough to see the people tending their fires, when I fell fast asleep. I was utterly exhausted, for in my anxiety to make a quick run home I had refused to let any of my men handle the sheet of my ship and had managed it myself without a break.

The crew seized this chance to discuss matters among themselves, and word went round that I was bringing home a fortune in gold and silver which the generous Aeolus son of Hippotas had given me. . . .

They undid the bag, the Winds all rushed out, and in an instant the tempest was upon them, carrying them headlong out to sea. They had good reason for their tears: Ithaca was vanishing astern.[vi]

From the Island of the Goats, hard by the land of the Cyclopes, the fleet rows to its next landfall, the Island of the Winds. And off the southeastern tip of Minorca, not far from the harbor of Mahón, its principal port, there is a small island known to this day as Isla del Aire, Spanish for "island of the wind." As Lita's photograph shows [19] this island seems to be sinking, as if it had once, using Ulysses' word, "floated" away from Minorca. Today, there is nothing on it except a lonely lighthouse, but it is not impossible that three thousand years ago Isla del Aire should have physically, or at least politically, formed part of Minorca itself, an island notorious for its interminable walls of dry yellow stone, which rise everywhere above its coast of sheer cliffs, and could well have suggested to Ulysses the "unbroken wall of bronze" below which "the cliffs rise sheer from the sea." [20] And seen from a small boat, that is, from below, Minorca itself also seems to float, for its base has eroded and is almost invisible in the clear waters. So I suggest that if Mallorca was the Island of the Cyclopes, its neighbor Minorca-Aire was Aiolos' home.

So much for Homer's description, which is brief. More interesting on this leg of our voyage is the fact that Ulysses sailed for nine days with Aiolos' west wind, from the Island of the Winds toward the east, and thought he was almost home before being blown back to Aiolia and its king's displeasure. Whereupon he rowed for six days, presumably in the same direction, and reached Telepylos. Now the other really long journey toward home described in *The Odyssey* lasts eighteen days, also to the east, from Ogygia to Scheria, which together with this leg adds up to a lot of sailing eastward. Even in magic numbers this led me right from the beginning to consider it probable that the land of the Cyclopes, which is Ulysses' turning point, must be further west than had usually been supposed. And this was what first brought me to the Balearics,

19. See photo page 87.
20. See photo page 88.

Minorcan *Naveta*

where I was happy to find an Island of Goats; any number of "residential" caves also used for sheltering sheep; one of the Mediterranean's greatest concentrations of neolithic remains apparently contemporary with implements from the era of Troy; an Island of the Winds; a still-surviving custom of piling stones above the high cliffs in interminable walls, which it does not take much of a sunset to "bronze"; and a people famous for their warlike use of these same stones, reminiscent of Polyphemos' last attack. And this westerly position of the Balearics within the Mediterranean allows me to propose an explanation for Ulysses' trip almost to Ithaka and back, an episode that has usually been dismissed as a dream or a myth.

If one sails a little south of east from Minorca, one passes between Sardinia and Tunis, and soon raises the Egadi Islands against the backdrop of western Sicily. This is not necessarily a nine days' sail, but I hope we agree that these were magic numbers, and it is still a medium distance on the scale of Ulysses' other passages, which range up to eighteen days. Now the sight of the Egadi and Sicily from the east is not too different from that of Cephalonia-Ithaka and the Peloponnese from the same direction,[21] so that considering the exhaustion that he is careful to describe, Ulysses could well have yielded to wishful thinking and confused the land he saw with the shores of his own kingdom, especially in the haze of an early morning or at twilight, and in the certainty that he was being sent home by a god. When the wind changed from west to east, a quick change not infrequent in these parts, he could have steered back to Aiolos, from whom he still hoped he could beg help the second time. But when Aiolos refused, Ulysses rowed away on his own, for the first time knowing exactly what course to steer for home: east.

It has even been suggested that Aiolos' leather bag of winds may have been the earliest map, drawn on a hide; an ingenious but rather far-

21. See photos pages 90 and 153.

Aiolos' Island, Isla del Aire, Minorca

The Coast of Bronze - minorca

88

fetched explanation that I will not argue for fear of becoming a wind-bag.[22] Be that as it may, Lita and I completed our inspection of the Balearics with a last look at Ibiza, then flew down the Spanish coast to Málaga, writing off that coast as beautiful in parts, but without a role in *The Odyssey*. But an amusing incident marked our stay in Málaga, capital of the Costa del Sol, Europe's new Miami Beach, which we found shrouded by a low cloud from the sea, the dampening effect of which was easily offset for the locals by bright billboards everywhere announcing next Sunday's bullfight with the great Cordobés.

When we were ready to leave, the cloud was still there, and though I knew the "shroud" was thin, having pierced it out of a blue sky before landing, I was obliged by regulations to file an instrument flight plan, a much lengthier process than my usual visual flight plan. While I was preparing this document, I was surprised by an excited and splendidly uniformed official who kept asking the tower to call an aircraft that was circling above the cloud, and order it to land, for the pilot was threatening to cancel his landing at Málaga and proceed elsewhere. Bureaucracy dealt with, Lita, I, our cameras, and our baggage were piled onto a tractor and driven to the inaccessible platform where private aircraft are customarily parked in Europe. And while we were loading up, a shiny new Beechcraft dropped out of the cloud, landed, and taxied to park next to us, where our friend the excited official waited. Out stepped "El Cordobés," followed by a small but decorative court, and all was explained. There is only one kind of pilot who would rather not land at his destination: a bullfighter, for whom landing means facing the bull, an enemy comparable to those who next greeted Ulysses.

22. "The scenes of the wanderings of Odysseus will be found," said Eratosthenes, "when you find the cobbler who sewed up the bag of the winds, and not before" (Sir John Sandys [I³–126]; see Bibliography).

The Egadi

THE WRATH OF
THE GODS

The Laistrygones' Telepylos *(Bonifacio)*

Circe's Aiaia *(Ischia)*

Hades *(The Caverns of Tangiers)*

Skylla, Charybdis, and the Trials *(Stromboli, Lipari, and Messina)*

THE LAISTRYGONES' TELEPYLOS
(Bonifacio)

We left the island and resumed our journey in a state of gloom; and the heart was taken out of my men by the wearisome rowing. . . .

For six days we forged ahead, never lying up even at night, and on the seventh we came to Telepylus, Lamus' stronghold in the Laestrygonian land, where shepherds bringing in their flocks at night hail and are answered by their fellows driving out at dawn. For in this land nightfall and morning tread so closely on each other's heels that a man who could do without sleep might earn a double set of wages, one as a neatherd and the other for shepherding white flocks of sheep. Here we found an excellent harbour, closed in on all sides by an unbroken ring of precipitous cliffs, with two bold headlands facing each other at the mouth so as to leave only a narrow channel in between. The captains of my squadron all steered their craft straight into the cover and tied up in the sheltered waters within. . . . But I did not follow them. Instead I brought my ship to rest outside the cove and made her fast with a cable to a rock at the end of the point. I then climbed the headland to get a view from the top, and took my bearings. No ploughed fields or other signs of human activities were to be seen: all we caught sight of was a wisp of smoke rising up from the countryside. So I sent a party inland to find out what sort of people the inhabitants were. . . .

Presently they fell in with a girl who was drawing water outside the village and for this purpose had come down to a bubbling spring called Artacie. . . . This strapping young woman proved to be the daughter of Antiphates, the Laestrygonian chief. . . . So they made their way to his house, and had no sooner gone in than they were confronted by Antiphates' wife, a creature of mountainous proportions, one glance at whom was enough to fill them with horror. The woman rushed off to the market-place to call her husband, Antiphates himself. And he gave my men a murderous reception, pouncing on one of them at once with a view to eating him for supper. The other two beat a hasty retreat and managed to make their way to the ships. Meanwhile Antiphates raised a hue and cry through the place, which brought the Laestrygonians running up from every side in their thousands—huge fellows, more like giants than men. Standing at the top of the cliffs they began pelting my flotilla with lumps of rock such as a man could barely lift; and the din that now rose from the ships, where the groans of dying men could be heard above the splintering of timbers, was appalling. One by one they harpooned their prey like fish and so carried them off to make their loathsome meal.[1]

We have established that Ulysses must have rowed east from Minorca, whence he thought he had earlier sailed east and all but reached home with Aiolos' wind. Now I submit that whereas he sailed with that wind somewhat south of east and passed below Sardinia to the Egadi and Sicily, mistaking them for home in his fatigue, he must now have rowed dead east, running squarely into Sardinia, which, in the cold light of those who have lost the protection of the gods, he now recognized as a foreign shore that lay across his route to Ithaka. And six days' rowing is not disproportionate to the nine days Ulysses had sailed with Aiolos' wind, if one compares the two distances. He could not know that beyond Sardinia there lay another and more formidable barrier—Italy—so he searched for a passage, and found it in the straits of Bonifacio, where the snug port of the same name awaited him, strikingly similar today to the harbor he describes.[1] But we are left with the problem of a land where night and day follow each other so closely. Note that our quotation says "nightfall and morning," whereas I have just said "night and day." Homer's words permit both translations, and this doubt, as well as the whole sentence itself, has given rise to all sorts of theories about this leg of the Odyssey. Proposed locations range from Scandinavia, where in summer nightfall and morning do indeed tread upon each other's heels, to my own tentative proposal of the tropics, where it is night that treads

1. See photo page 95.

The Port of the Laistrygones, Bonifacio

95

upon the heels of day with passionately meridional haste, leaving no room for twilight.

To send Ulysses to Scandinavia is not easy. The Pillars of Hercules at Gibraltar would have to become the midpoint of his Odyssey, instead of its occidental extreme; and once through them, both winds (the Portuguese trades) and current would be against this too long sail to the north, the aim of which would be difficult to explain. So it seemed much more sensible to me, if Ulysses had to be sent into the Atlantic, to have him sail south after Gibraltar, and to attempt for the first time, as far as I know, the "tropical" interpretation of the passage in question. At least this way the elements would be with him, just as they were with Columbus when he beat the Portuguese at their own game of discovery by sailing south before proceeding west to the New World, making friends of the easterly winds and currents of the southern part of the North Atlantic.[2] In history an advantage can easily turn into a handicap: possessing the Azores, the Portuguese used them as the starting point of all their attempts to sail west, and were therefore frustrated by the westerly winds and currents that dominate the North Atlantic. The easterly winds and currents that helped Columbus led me to surmise (having noted the distinction between discovering a continent and simply bumping into it) that the most likely candidates for having first bumped into America are not the Vikings, who certainly did so about the year 1000, but rather the Africans.[3]

The possibility of Ulysses' sailing south after Gibraltar must either be pursued or laid to rest, so I decided to fly down the Atlantic coast of Africa and around the Canary Islands, looking for a tropical Telepylos, which might encourage me to break once more with tradition and send Ulysses to the South Atlantic. Thence, God knows, I might have had to bring him all the way to the Antilles in order to have the winds and the

2. See endpaper charts.
3. My article in *El Tiempo* of Bogotá, October 12, 1968.

currents bring him back via the Azores. The names Kalypso and Charybdis would not have sounded strange in the Caribbean, and I might even have found encouragement in the recent revival of interest in a possible Phoenician landing in America, and in the "Cretan" White Gods of the Incas and Aztecs.[4] But fear not—that is not my conclusion.

As will be seen later, I do propose that Ulysses sail through the Pillars of Hercules, but not very far. But my flight to the Canaries illustrates once more the usefulness of my aircraft. Who would have traveled five thousand surface miles, off sea routes and beaten tracks, just to satisfy himself that the land of the Laistrygones is not to be found beyond Gibraltar? Yet that is just what *Oh Papa* enabled me to do in about twenty-five hours' flying time, keeping Lita and myself happily occupied for a mere week.

On our way to the Canaries, we landed at Marrakesh, a sudden paradise on the frontier of the desert and only a short hop from the coast, toward the crystal-clear backdrop of the Atlas Mountains. Here we stayed at one of the world's most charming hotels, for which we are indebted to the French Railroad Company of colonial days. Who can tell where beauty will bloom unheralded? We rested a couple of days, competing in horse-drawn carriages against roaring Vespas ridden by modern Moors to whom veiled women clung, en route perhaps to the enchanted gardens in which we also browsed, lulled by the song of birds and fountains; or to the bustling streets and squares where business and entertainment are still offered to all who will put up with heat and flies. Only an endless desert could preserve such a mixed Paradise.

Then we headed out toward the Canary Islands, helped by Columbus's east wind, which sometimes brings dust all the way from the Sahara, making a miniature desert in one's nostrils, as does the bone-dry *harmattan* of Nigeria. A low cloud covered the water and we seemed to

---

4. If you like far-out theories loosely reasoned, read Pierre Honoré (see Bibliography).

be suspended motionless above it while a distant jet passed swift and silent as a barracuda, giving me the feeling that, like Ulysses, I might end up alone in the "fish-infested sea," without knowing which way to turn. But I was soon relieved to find a hole in the overcast just where I figured the first Canary, Lanzarote, should be. I let down timidly and spotted land, a volcanic moonscape with a pretty port, from which we hopped to Lanzarote's twin, Fuerteventura, and on to Gran Canaria, which was to be our base. From there we flew all over the other islands, rounding Gomera, where nearly five hundred years ago the handsome widow of the Governor had waved godspeed to a still doubtful Discoverer; far-out Hierro; beautiful Palma; and the most varied of all, Tenerife, dominated by ten-thousand-foot Teide, king of the volcanoes of which each Canary has its share, as it does of beaches, deserts, oases, highland forests, white villages, and hotels full of refugees from dark Scandinavian winters. But I found no Telepylos, though we did have our little adventure when my baggage door flew open in midair and I had to return with a roaring Zephyr in my cabin.

Everything concerning the prehistory of these islands is tropically vague. The Guanches, their original inhabitants, are supposed to have shown in their physiognomy traces of Phoenician and of Greek, but upon inquiry one finds little authority for this romantic supposition. Pliny the Elder is supposed to have given them their name "The Fortunate Isles," which they certainly still are. And the ancient stone seals (*pintadas*), which are found only on Gran Canaria and can be seen there in a dusty museum overflowing with unmarked bones and stuffed animals, are supposed to be similar only to those found in Italy, Mexico, and Colombia. But this intriguing relationship does not seem to have been authoritatively established, nor any conclusions drawn. No, Telepylos must remain at Bonifacio.

There remains the poet's cryptic phrase about the shepherds of the night and those of the day, and before giving up both the Scandinavian and the tropical interpretations I investigated one more possibility. I feel sure that few of my readers will have noticed that there is one point within the Mediterranean that is as far south as the Canaries: our friend Arae Philenorum, at the bottom of the Gulf of Sirte. So on my Libyan flight I kept it in mind that if Telepylos could be placed there, it would tropically validate Homer's phrase about the day and the night. But after much cartographic juggling, I came to the conclusion that Philenia must remain the land of the Lotus-eaters and cannot be fitted into the Laistrygonian leg of the Odyssey any more than the Canaries can. Once again Bonifacio emerged victorious in its claim to the unflattering distinction of being the land of the fearsome Laistrygones, exactly where the second illustrated Ptolemy placed "Titani Port," the port of the giants,[5] on the narrow straits that separate Corsica from Sardinia. And in Lita's photo[6] of Bonifacio I think I can even see the rock where Ulysses moored his ship.

I can only suggest one possible explanation of Homer's phrase. In Corsica, as in the Balearics, sheep are often sheltered from the sun in caves, so that a shepherd leading his flock out of its shelter to graze in the cool of the evening might well encounter a herdsman bringing home the cattle from daytime pasture.

Two more coincidences support the traditional identification of Telepylos with Bonifacio. As late as 1910, Ferton,[7] said that Bonifacio's only supply of drinking water was still the fountain of Longone, outside the town and just about where Ulysses' men found Antiphates' daughter drawing water from Artakie. And there are plenty of neolithic remains from about the thirteenth century B.C. on both Corsica and Sardinia to connect this place with Minorca, the other Homeric land of stone-throwers.

5. Ptolomaeus, Ulm 1482 (see Bibliography).
6. See photo page 95.
7. Quoted by Mireaux (see Bibliography).

CIRCE'S AIAIA

(Ischia)

But while this massacre was still going on in the depths of the cover, I drew my sword from my hip, slashed through the hawser of my vessel, and yelled to the crew to dash in with their oars if they wished to save their skins. With the fear of death upon them they struck the water like one man, and with a sigh of relief we shot out to sea and left those frowning cliffs behind. My ship was safe. But that was the end of all the rest.

We travelled on in utter dejection, thankful to have escaped alive, but grieving for the good comrades we had lost. In due course we came to the island of Aeaea, the home of the beautiful Circe, a formidable goddess, though her voice is like a woman's. . . . We approached the coast of this island and brought our ship into the shelter of the haven without making a sound. Some god must have guided us in. And when we had disembarked, for two whole days and nights we lay on the beach, suffering not only from exhaustion but from the horrors we had been through.[ii]

True to character, Ulysses has acted alone, having taken the precaution of mooring outside the excellent harbor of Telepylos, so that his ship alone has survived the massacre that destroyed the rest of the squadron. Presumably he still thinks it was his homeland he saw when he first sailed east from the island of Aiolos with a godsent wind; but now he knows that in trying to row to the east without Aiolos' divine help he has made some mistake which he must urgently correct. Obviously he must still sail east, since dreadful Telepylos must lie between the Island of the Winds and Ithaka, which he has certainly not overshot. But is he north of his proper course or south of it?

For the first time Ulysses must pick a course by means other than "dead reckoning,"[8] and I propose that he must have used that primitive but excellent method of celestial navigation, latitude sailing, which the

8. Basically, heading and distance.

Polynesians used for centuries to pick their way from island to island across the lonely Pacific. This method consists simply of following the constant east-west track of a prominent star known to pass over one's destination. Longitude is a difficult concept to pin down without an accurate timepiece, so that huge errors in longitude were common even after the time of Columbus, who discovered America at least partly thanks to such an error, which made him place Asia just about where the New World lay. Ulysses must always solve the longitude question (whether to sail east or west) by dead reckoning, that is, by basing his reasoning on an assumption as to where he is, relative to where he wishes to go. In this case the obvious assumption is that he is still on the same side of Ithaka as Aiolos' island, so he must still sail east. But Ulysses is now definitely lost, having failed to row home along the same course he followed earlier with the help of Aiolos' wind, and he admits it by confessing that he can no longer tell where the sun will rise or set. He must therefore decide whether to sail north or south (of east) by the latitude method, and several passages in *The Odyssey* show that he knows his constellations and their stars, and uses them for direction. That he and his ancestors before him have surely noticed which stars pass directly above Ithaka in their nightly journey from east to west is clearly borne out by his reference, once after Skylla and again at Eumaios' hut, to the "zenith of the stars."

Now it happens that the stars which then passed directly over Ithaka, give or take the few degrees of error permissible in observations with the naked eye, included half the best navigational stars chosen for the Northern Hemisphere by our modern air almanac, among them the three brightest of the first magnitude: Arcturus in the constellation of Boötes, Vega in Lira, and Capella in Auriga.[9] Given this fortunate circumstance

9. See chart page 102. The others are Deneb in Cygnus, Marfak in Perseus, and Castor in Gemini, making a total of six out of the twelve listed in the almanac. For the uninitiated to check this, it may first be necessary to read Chapter V and understand that Ulysses' pole was not ours, so that the stars that "overheaded" Ithaka then are not those that do so now.

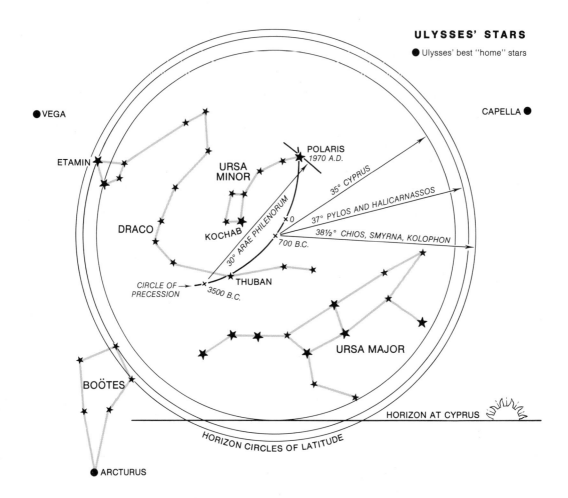

ULYSSES' STARS

● Ulysses' best "home" stars

VEGA

CAPELLA ●

ETAMIN

POLARIS
1970 A.D.

URSA
MINOR

35° CYPRUS

37° PYLOS AND HALICARNASSOS

DRACO

38½° CHIOS, SMYRNA, KOLOPHON

KOCHAB

30° ARAE PHILENORUM

0

700 B.C.

CIRCLE OF
PRECESSION

3500 B.C.

THUBAN

URSA MAJOR

BOÖTES

HORIZON AT CYPRUS

HORIZON CIRCLES OF LATITUDE

● ARCTURUS

and the fact that Bonifacio is the northernmost point in all his voyage, Ulysses has only to note that these "home" stars pass to the south of his present latitude to decide that Ithaka lies to the southeast of his position. So we can trust him to row somewhat south of east from Bonifacio, which brings him naturally to Ischia, where I propose to place the home of Circe.

But first I must deal with Cape Circeo, which is supposed to have borne the name of the sorceress from the time of Strabo, though we have seen that the first two atlases with maps both omit it. To me Cape Circeo is right neither in position, for it is dead east of Bonifacio, nor in description, and Ulysses' description is quite precise: thrice he calls Aiaia an island, adding for good measure: "When I climbed to a craggy outlook I found that this is an island, and for the most part low lying, the boundless deep circling it like a crown." [iii] Lita's photograph [10] shows today's Cape Circeo and the marshes that unite it to the continent, which have sometimes been cited as an explanation of Ulysses' having seen the sea on all sides. But aside from this lame explanation, what about "for the most part low lying"? As the photograph shows, Circeo is a vertical rock. To me it seems more logical for Ulysses to sail, not dead east, but clearly south of east, after so painfully discovering his mistake at Bonifacio and therefore checking his stars, and so reach a real island, Ischia, from the high center of which one can observe exactly the sort of panorama he describes.[11] Nor do I find it unlikely that later generations should have named after Circe the most prominent cape near her home island, while the island itself finally adopted another name. We have already seen that historical names are nomads, and, for good measure, *Atlas Antiquus* [12] has Ischia marked "Aenaria I.," which is not unlike "Aiaia."

The objection can be made that in sailing from Bonifacio to Ischia,

10. See photo page 104.
11. See photo page 106. Unfortunately only the high side of the island is visible.
12. Kiepert (see Bibliography).

Cape Circeo

Ulysses might first have seen high Cape Circeo, and probably would have seen Ponza and its neighboring islands. This is true but no objection, for Ulysses does not say that his first sight of land after Telepylos was Aiaia, but on the contrary that he reached Aiaia "in due course." And after his tragic experience in the land of the Laistrygones he would hardly have been inclined to land on the cape of an unknown continent, but would probably be looking for an island more likely to provide food (principally game) than tight little Ponza and its tiny neighbors. So Ischia seems to me to fill the bill in every way, and I suggest that Ulysses sailed silently onto one of the beaches near Laco Ameno, on the northwest corner of the island.

It is near here that archaeologists from Naples and from the University Museum of Philadelphia have uncovered an acropolis and a necropolis belonging to eighth-century Pithekoussai, part of the oldest Greek colony yet located in the West. The name means "place of apes" and fits Circe's Aiaia, which is a veritable circus of animals. The necropolis contains several crematory mounds, of which Dr. Giorgio Buchner, director of the project, says the following:

The remains consisting of the ashes of carbonized wood mixed with fragments of burnt human bones, pottery, and personal ornaments were carried to the burial place and heaped on the surface. In addition, an unburnt wine jug was often placed on the heap of ashes. The whole was then concealed beneath a tumulus of rough stones, with a diameter between 1.50 and 4.50 meters, in a fashion unfamiliar in Greek burials except in parts of East Greece. All the more interesting to note is the close correspondence of the Pithekoussan Tumuli with the tombs described by Homer, particularly the tomb of Patroclus (Iliad XXIII-255 f.), naturally taking into consideration that Patroclus' tomb was that of a hero, and these are only the tombs of ordinary mortals. The function of the unburnt jug as well can be explained by reference to Homer (Iliad XXII-250) as the jug used to quench with wine the embers of the funeral pyre.[13]

13. Giorgio Buchner (see Bibliography).

Circe's Ischia

We are reminded of Elpenor's request to Ulysses, who meets him in Hades after the young sailor has fallen off Circe's roof, full of the sorceress's good wine, and broken his neck. "Burn me there [in Aiaia] with all my armour, and heap a mound for me on the shore of the grey sea, and fix on the mound the oar I rowed with." [iv] It almost seems as if Homer had visited the unfamiliar mounds of Pithekoussai, and one imagines the wily Ulysses keeping Elpenor's oar as a spare and planting the unfortunate young drinker's jug on top of the pyre instead. Moreover one of the cups found in an Ischian grave is a very special one, for it bears the following inscription (translated by John Boardman): "Nestor had a most drinkworthy cup, but whoever drinks of mine will straightforward be smitten with desire of faircrowned Aphrodite." Buchner dates the cup and its inscription around 700 B.C., making it one of the oldest documents in Greek script and the first piece of poetry of Homeric times preserved in contemporary writing. As if this reference to Nestor and to precisely the type of potion that Circe gave Ulysses were not enough, a seal was also found on Ischia, which shows Ajax carrying the body of Achilles from under the city wall of Troy, a story told neither in *The Iliad* nor in *The Odyssey*.

The first thing Ulysses does after regaining his breath is kill a huge stag on which he and his crew feast for a whole day, but matters are not to remain that simple. The scouts dispatched to make contact with Circe, whose "castle of dressed stone" Ulysses has spotted by its plume of smoke, are unceremoniously transformed into grunting swine. Their leader, Eurylochos, who has followed Ulysses' Laistrygonian example by watching from the outside, returns to the good black ship to tell the horrible story, and his suggestion is to "leave ill enough alone." But Ulysses likes to be loyal to his men whenever the odds are not overwhelmingly against such a course—especially when it means facing a woman, however witchy—and as usual, his daring is rewarded. Hermes himself, "looking like a young man in the full charm of youth when the down first starts to show" [v] falls in with him on the way and tells him how to overcome the beautiful sorceress and become master of her bed (and board) for a whole year. Indeed, Ulysses' stay might have been longer had not his crew reminded him of home, and had not Circe agreed to show the way, much as she would have loved to retain him, "but not against his wishes," [vi] says she.

Before leaving Aiaia, I want to mention that for a time, while I was still wondering if Ulysses might not have sailed to northern Europe, I tried to identify Circe with a Nordic witch, surrounded as she was by deer and boar. Then the northern sun could easily have confused Ulysses, the fogbound Kimmerians to whom she sent him could have lived in a London pea soup, and Skylla on the Scilly Isles. But again, as in the case of Bonifacio, this far-out theory had to be discarded, principally for reasons of navigation.[14] In any case, one thing is clear: Ulysses, who thus far has tried to guess more or less where he is, now finally admits that he is quite lost. "My friends," he says, "East and West mean nothing to us now." [vii]

We of *Oh Papa* flew from Bonifacio to Ponza and the neighboring islands, thence to Cape Circeo, and finally over Ischia to Naples, where I was directed to park my plane in a little meadow of wildflowers. We found the great port more beautiful than ever, and teeming with pleasant liars who tried to "do us in" on everything from gasoline taxes to landing fees, all of which seemed to start at three thousand lire but finally fell to a level determined only by our resistance and good humor. I cannot tell whether it was the ancient spell of Circe or my growing familiarity with ever-victorious Ulysses, but the fact is that I left with the feeling of having held my own in all the haggling, which makes as good a souvenir as any. When I finally took off, I was almost charmed enough to carry out exactly the old injunction: "See Naples and die. . . ."

14. Try Gilbert Pillot and see if he convinces you (see Bibliography).

HADES
(The Caverns of Tangiers)

Thus she brought us to the deep-flowing River of Ocean and the frontiers of the world, where the fog-bound Cimmerians live in the City of Perpetual Mist. . . .

Here we beached our boat and after disembarking the sheep made our way along the banks of the River of Ocean till we reached the spot that Circe had described. There . . . [I] dug a trench about a cubit long and a cubit wide. Around this trench I poured libations to all the dead, first with mingled honey and milk, then with sweet wine, and last of all with water. Over all this I sprinkled some white barley, and then began my prayers to the helpless ghosts of the dead, promising them that directly I got back to Ithaca I should sacrifice a barren heifer in my palace, the best I had in my possession, and heap the pyre with treasures, and make Teiresias a separate offering of the finest jet-black sheep to be found in my flocks. When I had finished my prayers and invocations to the communities of the dead, I took the sheep and cut their throats over the trench so that the dark blood poured in. And now the souls of the dead who had gone below came swarming up from Erebus—fresh brides, unmarried youths, old men with life's long suffering behind them, tender young girls still nursing this first anguish in their hearts, and a great throng of warriors killed in battle, their spear-wounds gaping yet and all their armour stained with blood. From this multitude of souls, as they fluttered to and fro by the trench, there came a moaning that was horrible to hear. Panic drained the blood from my cheeks. I turned to my comrades and told them quickly to flay the sheep I had slaughtered with my sword and burn them, while they prayed to the gods, to mighty Hades and august Persephone. But I myself sat on guard, bare sword in hand, and prevented any of the feckless ghosts from approaching the blood before I had speech with Teiresias.[viii]

Set up your mast, spread the white sail and sit down in the ship. The North Wind will blow her on her way; and when she has brought you across the

River of Ocean, you will come to a wild coast and to Persephone's Grove, where the tall poplars grow and the willows that so quickly shed their seeds. Beach your boat there by Ocean's swirling stream and march on into Hades' Kingdom of Decay. There the River of Flaming Fire and the River of Lamentation, which is a branch of the Waters of Styx, unite round a pinnacle of rock to pour their thundering streams into Acheron. This is the spot, my lord, that I bid you to seek out. . . .

Presently the prophet himself will come to you, my lord king. And he will lay down for you your journey and the distances to be covered, and direct you home across the fish-delighting seas.[ix]

Circe's instructions for reaching Hades are quite precise, and to start from Ischia on his trip toward the River of Ocean, for which I have already proposed Gibraltar, what Ulysses needs is precisely a good northeaster. As we have also seen, Boreas, the wind that Circe promises, can lie anywhere between northeast and northwest. So, based on the Homeric view of the globe, I felt little doubt that "the deep-flowing River of Ocean and the frontiers of the world" were to be found at the Straits of Gibraltar, especially remembering that Ulysses, upon finding Elpenor in Hades, exclaims: "Elpenor, how did you come here, under the Western gloom?" [x] and that the ghost of Ulysses' mother, Antikleia, uses exactly the same expression. What could be further west to a Mycenaean than the Pillars of Hercules? But I was worried about locating the fog-bound Kimmerians and their City of Perpetual Mist so close to Málaga, today's sun capital of Europe, until to my surprise I found Málaga under the low cloud blown in from the sea by Circe's wind. That pall, often occurring in September or October, covered Málaga during the three days of our stay and very nearly cost the Malagueños their Sunday bullfight, as I mentioned before.

Four times Lita and I had pierced that cloud: twice on landing and takeoff and twice when driving to and from the lovely mountaintop village of Mijas, which is a good antidote to the rapid Miami-Beaching of the Costa del Sol, complete with ancient free-form bullring and taxi donkeys. And the cloud persisted all the way to Gibraltar, where Lita photographed its tail end against the famous Rock,[15] while I happily infringed on a maze of Spanish and British "forbidden areas," which attempt to carry the old dispute over the Rock into the limitless sky and through which one is not supposed to fly. Over the water there was a break in the cloud, and then the African coast from Tangiers south was again shrouded, all the way down to the Canaries.

During the second autumn of the Odyssey, Ulysses, with his godsent wind, must have sailed into the straits against the current, beached his boat, and continued by land along the shore of the River of Ocean until he came to the spot described by Circe. Today, if one sails a small boat into the straits with a northeaster, and looks for a good place to beach, one will most likely choose one of the pebbly beaches of Tangiers. And if one continues by land along the coast toward Cape Espartel, one soon comes upon a devilish panorama of volcanic caves that to this day bear mythological names. And this "Hades" appears suddenly, right after the woods that shade the western suburbs of the old International City, which overlook the beach where one has left one's boat. So, in the days of Ulysses, "Persephone's Grove" could easily have been adjacent on the west to a volcanic "River of Flaming Fire and Lamentation," and I feel justified in placing Hades in a volcanic cave such as the one Lita photographed.[16] We were interested to see that the Arabs still cut millstones out of the walls of the cave, leaving a pattern in the rock very similar to the "wavy" stucco so typical of Moorish ornamentation.

In accordance with our estimate of Ulysses' speed with godsent winds, to sail direct from Ischia to Gibraltar would take about five days and nights each way. But since most of the course lies along the North African coast, I am inclined to think that Ulysses probably slept ashore whenever possible, and that the whole journey probably took him about

15. See photo page 112.
16. See photo page 115.

Gibraltar, the Land of the Kimmerians

three weeks. This is a long trip, but not too long for Ulysses under orders from a goddess, and *The Odyssey* does not fix any particular duration.

Before leaving the subject of the location of Hades, it is worth pointing out, as noted by Bradford, that even to the Phoenicians the Rock of Gibraltar (Calpe) and Mount Hacko, its African counterpart, were known as the Pillars of Melkrath, whom mythologists identify with Herakles (or Hercules), both connected with the underworld. To me, myths whose pre-Homeric origin cannot be clearly established are not basis enough for identification, because, as I have pointed out, most post-Homeric myths more probably have their origin in contemporary interpretations of Homer's geography than vice versa. But once an identification has been reached by other means, a supporting myth is nice to find. And the cave we photographed is to this day known as Hercules' Grotto.

In *The Odyssey*'s Book of the Dead there are enough myths for everyone, and those interested in mythology should read it carefully. There is no space for details here, but among the tens of thousands of "disembodied ghosts who [according to Achilles] live on here without their wits," and who throng around Ulysses waiting to drink the sacrificial blood in order to be able to communicate with the living, we cannot forget Ulysses' own mother Antikleia, who gives him his first news of home, and so perhaps revives the yearning for family, and above all for vengeance, that will drive him toward Ithaka yet another seven years. Theban Teiresias, Prince of Seers, warns Ulysses of trials still to come, and foresees an inland Odyssey for him even after his return to Ithaka, to a land where men cannot tell "an oar from a winnowing-fan." [xi] Is this Homer's plan for a future poem of adventure that will take Ulysses into southern Russia? Unfortunately this poem was never composed, or, if composed, was lost. "As for your own end," Teiresias adds, "Death will come to you out of the sea, Death in his gentlest guise. When he takes you, you will be worn out after an easy old age and surrounded by prosperous people." [xii] One more reason for persevering toward home.

Next Ulysses' mother comes, followed by "all the women who had been the wives and daughters of princes," most of whom claim to have been loved by gods, thus giving divine origin to many Mycenaean heroes, such as Nestor. Then Agamemnon, King of Men, reports his tragic end at the hands of his wife Klytaimnestra and her lover, and gives Ulysses two pieces of very sound advice: "Never be too gentle even with your wife, nor show her all that is in your mind," and "Do not sail openly into port when you reach your own country." Finally Ulysses hails Achilles himself as a "mighty prince even among the dead," Achilles' reply to which summarizes the Greeks' very sensible attitude toward death: "Ulysses, my lord, spare me your praise of Death. If I could only return to earth, I would rather be the serf of some landless man, who himself has little enough to live on, than king of all these dead men whose lives are done." [xiii]

Ulysses' return from Hades to Aiaia makes just as much navigational sense as his outward trip. Here is his description:

> I made off quickly to my ship and told my men to embark and loose the hawsers. They climbed in at once and took their seats on the benches, and the current carried her down the River of Ocean, helped by our oars at first and later by a friendly breeze.
>
> From the flowing waters of the River of Ocean my ship passed into the wide spaces of the open sea, and so reached Aeaea, the Island of the Rising Sun, where tender Dawn has her home and her dancing-lawns. [xiv]

Note that this time it is not the wind that brings Ulysses "across" the current as on the way out, but the current itself, helped by oars, that carries him "down" the River of Ocean and into the "wide spaces" of the Mediterranean, where a friendly breeze out of the west takes over the task of returning him to the Island of the Rising Sun, and therefore east and into the arms of Circe. This is precisely the current that helped us locate the River of Ocean within our picture of Homer's world, and it is the same surface current that in the Second World War allowed

Hades, Cape Espartel

Germany's submariners to enter the Mediterranean without power so as to escape detection by the British on the Rock. The only thing the Germans discovered that might have been new to Ulysses was the opposite underwater current that falls deep into the Atlantic off the submerged cliff formed by the western extreme of the floor of the straits. On it the Germans rode their deadly tin sharks silently out of Ulysses' sea, as silently as they had entered it. To each age its own form of hell.

We of *Oh Papa* were delighted to land at Tangiers' pleasant, small airport, where we were impressed by the quick intelligence of a race of Moroccans more used to international status than to Moslem reserve. So international, in fact, is Tangiers that when in the evening I sat at one of the world's most amusing sidewalk cafés, watching veils follow miniskirts and fezzes Panamas, the waiter said to Lita, who arrived late: "There is your husband, or whatever he may be . . ."

SKYLLA, CHARYBDIS, AND THE TRIALS
(Stromboli, Lipari, and Messina)

On their return to Aiaia from the halls of Hades, Ulysses' men take a well-earned rest of the sort they prefer: they feast for twenty-four hours on Circe's good game and wine, while Ulysses lies beside his sorceress for the last time, tells her of his visit to the underworld, and hears her sailing directions for the next leg of his trip:

Your next encounter will be with the Sirens, who bewitch everybody that approaches them. There is no home-coming for the man who draws near them unawares and hears the Sirens' voices . . . as they sit there in a meadow piled high with the mouldering skeletons of men, whose withered skin still hangs upon their bones. Drive your ship past the spot, and to prevent any of your crew from hearing, soften some beeswax and plug their ears with it. But if you wish to listen yourself, make them bind you hand and foot on board and stand you up by the step of the mast, with the rope's ends lashed to the mast itself.[xv]

From Circe's point of view this will be the last female voice to try to hold Ulysses, and she is certainly not going to let another woman succeed where she herself has failed; hence her careful instructions to her always curious lover, whose ears she has no hope of stopping. Little does she know that Kalypso the nymph and Navsikaa the girl are yet to come. Apart from the instructions, Homer does not give us much of a description, but if one is to sail from Ischia to Ithaka, one must certainly first head southeast along the Italian coast—although not, I think, into the Gulf of Naples, where Vesuvius grumbles, but rather across it, where the next landfall will be Capri, an island toward which sirens have always been inclined for reasons that I think show well in Lita's photo,[17] especially toward Marina Piccola, which still faces the *scoglio delle Sirene*. Our faithful Ptolemy-Crivelli of 1477 writes "Sirenum" under Capri, my choice for the home of the Sirens. Their Temptation of Knowledge, so reminiscent of the Biblical Tree, Ulysses manages to evade by the means Circe has prescribed, even though they sing "Come hither illustrious Ulysses, flower of Achean heroes, and do you allow your ship to rest so that you may listen to our voices. We know all that the Argives and Trojans suffered in wide Troy, and we know all that is going to happen on this fruitful earth." [xvi]

Once past Capri, the route is just as obvious. Ulysses must follow the Italian coast as far as Cape Vaticano, and there make his choice: west toward Stromboli's volcano with its neighboring isles and around the western end of Sicily, or south through the Strait of Messina. Circe's instructions are so true, that like the Navy all I can say is, "Now hear this":

When your crew have carried you past this danger you will have reached a point beyond which I cannot fully guide you. Two ways will lie before you, and you must choose between them as you see fit, though I will tell you both. One leads to those sheer cliffs which the blessed gods know as the Wandering

17. See photo page 118.

The Sirens' Capri

Rocks. Here blue-eyed Amphitrite sends her great breakers thundering in, and the very birds cannot fly by in safety. Even from the shy doves that bring ambrosia to Father Zeus the beetling rock takes toll each time they pass. . . .

In the other direction lie two rocks, the higher of which rears its sharp peak up to the very sky and is capped by black clouds that never stream away. . . . But half-way up the crag there is a misty cavern, facing the West and running down to Erebus, past which, my lord Odysseus, you must steer your ship. The strongest bowman could not reach the gaping mouth of the cave with an arrow shot from a ship below. It is the home of Scylla, the creature with the dreadful bark. . . . She has twelve feet . . . and six long necks, each ending in a grisly head with triple rows of teeth, set thick and close, and darkly menacing death. Up to her middle she is sunk in the depths of the cave, but her heads protrude from the fearful abyss, and thus she fishes from her own abode . . . [and] from every passing vessel she snatches a man with each of her heads and so bears off her prey.

The other of the two rocks is lower, as you, Odysseus, will see, and the distance between them is no more than a bowshot. A great fig-tree with lux-uriant foliage grows upon the crag, and it is below this that dread Charybdis sucks the dark waters down. Three times a day she spews them up, and three times she swallows them down once more in her horrible way. Heaven keep you from the spot when she is at her work, for not even the Earthshaker could save you from disaster. No: you must hug Scylla's rock and with all speed drive your ship through, since it is far better that you should have to mourn the loss of six of your company than that of your whole crew. . . .

And call on Cratais, Scylla's mother, who brought her into the world to prey on men. She will prevent her from making a second sally.[xvii]

Without even discussing it further, Ulysses accepts Circe's "Hobson's choice" and sails with the wind past Skylla's rock, just as any sailor would have done. Why brave Stromboli's fire and the Wandering Rocks in order to sail by far the longer of the two courses (counter-clockwise around Sicily)?

With modern conceit I flew closer to Stromboli than even Zeus's own

Stromboli, the Rock Over Which Zeus's Doves Do Not Dare to Fly

doves had dared, and my recognition of Circe's words was a delight.[18] But I had some doubts whether the Wandering Rocks could be identified with the Lipari (or Eole) Islands until I flew low around them. The sight of these islands, stretching away into the dusk like a squadron of ghostly caravels, convinced me that they did indeed seem to float in the Mare Tirreno, and I hope Lita's photograph [19] will serve as proof. For those who prefer a more detailed explanation, it has been pointed out that Isola Salina, in the center of the group, is to this day a source of light pumice stone, large pieces of which often become detached from the shore and "wander" away upon the water.

As to Skylla and Charybdis, I tried all sorts of alternatives but found none to compare with their traditional location at the Strait of Messina.[20] True, it would be difficult today to shoot an arrow across the water, and Circe is quite definite in stating that the distance between the two rocks is no more than a bowshot. So I surmise either that she is exaggerating in order to make sure that wayward Ulysses will stick close to the lesser of the two dangers, or else that currents and volcanic disturbances have widened the strait considerably during the last three thousand years.

The ingenious suggestion has been made that Skylla might be Etna, and her necks flows of lava, a particularly neat rationalization in view of Skylla's mother's name, Kratais. Even though Skylla's cave would then have to face east instead of west, I climbed Etna to have a look, but I still consider it unnecessary to seek an extraordinary explanation for a sea monster the like of which sailors have described throughout history. Columbus himself was reminded of one in the strait between Trinidad and the mainland, and named the place "Boca de la Sierpe." The fish-infested waters of Messina are especially propitious for such visions, which landlubbers (or airlubbers like me) may doubt but can never

18. See photo page 120.
19. See photo page 122.
20. See photo page 124.

The Floating Rocks, Isole Lipari

totally dispel. And here is the comment of an expert:

[Homer's] description strongly recalls an octopus hiding in its lair; for it sometimes anchors itself with two of its tentacles, and uses the other six to catch its prey. The ends of the tentacles, usually rolled up on themselves, are very like heads and the "three rows of thickset crowded fangs" may well refer to the rows of suckers on the tentacles, even though they are not actually triple. Moreover, though an octopus has no voice, it may make an absurd noise with its siphon when it is out of the water and sound like a yelping puppy. Skylla may thus be an octopus, but on a Homeric scale.[21]

So Homer's Skylla can stay where tradition has kept her.

As to Charybdis, let us see what modern sailing directions advise: *Routes de la Mediterranée pour le Yachting*[22] says that to sail southward through the strait with the wind blowing from the north and an opposite stream, it is wise to stay near the shore of Calabria as far as Villa San Giovanni, then go back toward Cape Scaletta, in Sicily, south of Messina; and adds that when the winds are strong, one may have difficulties even with the help of an engine. And *Sailing Directions for the Mediterranean*[23] points out that, in summer, winds normally blow from the northeast from morning to sunset, but clouds on the mountains of Calabria foretell strong winds blowing from the southeast. So here is the selfsame north wind that Circe gave Ulysses to bring him from Ischia to Messina; her instructions to stay close to Skylla (Calabria) rather than Charybdis; the difficulty of the passage even for a modern yacht with an engine; and Circe's black clouds, which, capping Calabrian Skylla, warn of the coming change of wind that will keep Ulysses on the eastern shore of Sicily for a whole month. The conditions described prevail in June, which makes it probable that Ulysses left Circe in spring, all the more painful for the lovelorn sorceress.

The *Sailing Directions* also detail for us the character of Charybdis

21. Bernard Heuvelmans, p. 46 (see Bibliography).
22. P. M. Bourdeaux, Tome I, p. 17 (see Bibliography).
23. U.S.H.O. II, 8-3, 4.

Skylla and Charybdis, the Straits of Messina

herself when they warn that at places where the currents encounter changes in the depth of the strait, or where they meet the central current and countercurrents, whirlpools (*garofoli*) are formed. Among the special places where *garofoli* form, Torre di Faro is mentioned, thus neatly locating Charybdis across the strait from Skylla. One more detail is also pretty close to Circe: currents and their resultant whirlpools are said to reverse themselves several times a day.

Though Ulysses, disregarding Circe, dons his armor and prepares to sell his men's lives as dear as possible, Skylla's toll of six is paid in order to avoid Charybdis' whirlpool, and once through the strait the black-prowed ship is soon beached against the storm in a sheltered cove on the eastern shore of Sicily.

> Your next landfall will be the island of Thrinacie, where the Sun-god pastures his large herds and well-fed sheep. . . . [T]o shepherd them they have goddesses, the lovely Nymphs, Phaethusa and Lampetie, children of Hyperion the Sun-god. . . . But if you hurt them, then I swear to you that your ship and your company will be destroyed. And if you yourself contrive to escape, you will come home late, in evil plight, with all your comrades lost.[xviii]

Who will doubt that Sicily is well-named Thrinakia, the triangular isle, whose armorial crest still bears three running legs, and on whose eastern shore the Piana di Catania still contains the best grazing lands? The Sun God is never long absent from these shores, as all English tourists know, though he would do better now with a refinery than with all his precious cattle.[24] Also amusing is the similarity between the names of the nymphs and that of nearby Lampedusa. Anyhow, Eurymachos, the ship's troublemaker, who failed to thwart Ulysses on Aiaia, now succeeds. And Ulysses, who never fights unnecessarily against overwhelming odds, allows his exhausted and mutinous crew to rest on Thrinakia while the storm rages, after extracting from them a promise

24. See photo page 127.

to spare the Sun God's cattle. But the storm lasts a month and rations run low, and while Ulysses sleeps Eurymachos convinces the men to feast on the forbidden meat.

All Ulysses can do is put to sea as soon as possible, and his words are again quite definite for our identifications, for he says that the storm kept him ashore with its south wind, the *sirocco* still forecast today by clouds over Calabria, and exactly the wind that would have kept any sailor from starting out of Catania for Ithaka in a square-rigged boat. So, when Ulysses finally raises his white sail, we must assume that he at last has a wind out of the west or northwest, and sails east for home as he has been trying to do ever since Aiolos' isle. But one does not slaughter a god's cattle with impunity:

When we had left the island astern and no other land, nor anything but sky and water was to be seen, Zeus brought a sombre cloud to rest above the ship so that the sea was darkened by its shadow. Before she had run very far, a howling wind suddenly sprang up from the west and hit us with hurricane force. The squall snapped both forestays together. As the mast fell aft, all the rigging tumbled into the bilge, and the mast itself, reaching the stern, struck the helmsman on the head and smashed in all the bones of his skull. He plunged like a diver from the poop, and his brave soul left his body. Then at one and the same moment Zeus thundered and struck the vessel by lightning. The whole ship reeled to the blow of his bolt and was filled with sulphur.[xix]

The reality of this description is overwhelming, and yet there is something wrong. Was not Ulysses sailing east? How then could the west wind snap the forestays and lay the mast aft across the helmsman's skull? As far as I know, this fact has confused all who have tried to make sense out of this passage, but after much thought, I think I have a simple explanation to offer. If we look at a map, we see that from the western shore of Sicily, in his haste to reach Ithaka before the offended god strikes back, Ulysses has embarked on one of those "lonely passages" which he is usually at pains to avoid. Then, when the black cloud settles above his ship, he knows he cannot make it, and hope-

Hyperion's Cattle Country in Thrinakia, near Catania

lessly plays his last card. He turns back toward the shore, resigned to working his way along the "sole of the boot" of Italy as far as the gods will let him. This is why, before he gets very far, Zeus's lightning catches him heading west. And *Pour le Yachting* says that before leaving Messina for Greece it is indispensable to get very precise meteorological information, for if it is adverse "you will not get very far." [25]

All is now lost, and only Ulysses survives, lashed with the leather backstay to what is left of mast and keel. The south wind rises again, dragging him back towards Charybdis, which shows that we are right in supposing that he was south of the straits when the cloud first descended. At dawn Ulysses is in the clutches of the whirlpool, and manages to survive once more only by hanging on to the fig tree while the waters swallow and regurgitate his improvised "life raft." Then for nine days more he drifts across the sea, until on the dark night of the tenth the gods wash him up on the isle of Ogygia, home of the fair Kalypso, whose charms he will enjoy for the next seven years, even to satiety.

Having flown from Naples to Stromboli, *Oh Papa* nosed low into the Strait of Messina, practically skimming the water but still safe from Skylla and Charybdis. Or so I thought until it was nearly too late, and I had virtually to stand *Oh Papa* on her tail to avoid an aerial cable that now joins Sicily to Calabria but was not indicated on my map. Each must face his own dangers; so, like Ulysses, I stuck to my course and flew all the way out to Ustica, where Bradford has placed Aiolos. But, as I have already said, from Ustica Ulysses would not have had room for so much sailing east, nor would he have had reason to sail to Bonifacio. Then I flew on to the Egadi Islands in front of Mount Erix, western Sicily's Mountain of Mysteries, which I had climbed before. This is a traditional location for the land of the Cyclopes, which I can-

25. P. M. Bourdeaux, Tome I, p. 67 (see Bibliography).

not accept for the same reason (too far east), and also because Minorca fits much better.

As dusk began to fall I headed for Palermo, with my gas indicator nearing zero, but certainly not anticipating any complications. Nevertheless, complications came in the form of a prolonged discussion in Italian over the radio as to whether I should land at Punta Raisi International Airport or at Bocca di Falco in town. And when I finally made it to Bocca, practically in the dark, without runway lights, and on my last gallon of gas, I got quite a reception from the local authorities. But all ended well, and while Lita was shown to the Aeroclub's powder room (locally known as the *palazzetto*) I had to stretch my fractured Italian, which, in an emergency, I fabricate out of a sort of "pidgin" Spanish, to tape an interview about the world's lightplane speed record which I had established in Bogotá not long before. Then we repaired to one of the world's most beautiful hotels, the Villa Egea, and danced away the night on a terrace overlooking Palermo's wonderful bay, ready to take off next morning for the land of Kalypso the nymph.

REPRIEVE, TEMPTATION, AND REVENGE

Kalypso's Ogygia and East *(Malta)*

Navsikaa's Scheria *(Cyprus)*

Ithaka *(still Ithaka)*

KALYPSO'S OGYGIA AND EAST
(Malta)

To Kalypso's island of Ogygia, where Ulysses is finally washed ashore, Homer brings us on Hermes' winged sandals of untarnishable gold. "From the upper air he stepped onto the Pierian range, and thence he swooped down on the sea and sped over the waves, as the cormorant drenches its thick plumage in the brine when it plunges after fish down the desolate gulfs of the unharvested deep, till he reached the faraway island of Ogygia in the violet sea." [i]

Oh Papa's sandals were not golden, but over the straits that separate Sicily and Africa, and after checking Pantelleria, we did in fact swoop down out of the clouds that covered the shy Pelagie islands (Linosa and Lampedusa) to skim the waves that foam around Malta. So close to the "desolate gulfs of the unharvested deep" did we fly on our first reconnaissance of the three Maltese islands (Malta, Comino, and Gozo) that the British air traffic controller who had authorized our flight suddenly cried, "Where are you, sir, radar has lost you. . . ." [1]

After seven years on the island, Ulysses spends his days weeping for home, though at night he still sleeps "in the hollow cave, cold lover beside an ardent nymph no longer pleasing in his eyes." [ii] This development is undoubtedly right, but still a little sad in view of the beautiful Kalypso's desperate efforts to hold Ulysses' love by offering him immortality. And Ulysses' refusal reminds one of Kierkegaard's "What man really loves is finitude." Hermes, sent by Zeus at Athena's request, to order "dainty" Kalypso to give up her lover, describes his journey from Olympos "over so great a space of sea, without any nearby city where

1. See photo page 134.

Malta, Kalypso's Ogygia

men sacrifice to the gods"; [iii] and the remote island he finally reaches is described as a paradise of juniper, cedar, alder, aspen, and cypress, alive with horned owl, falcon, and birds of the coast, where the entrance to Kalypso's great cavern is garlanded with vines and gladdened by four crystal rivulets that run across a soft meadow of iris and parsley.

This description made me doubt at first whether Ogygia could be Malta, sun-baked as Castille in summer, its noble churches, palaces, and fortresses the same color as its thirsty earth. But we landed and went to the old hotel overlooking Valetta's multiple harbor, guarded by the forts (reminiscent of our own Cartagena de Indias) where the knights withstood the Great Siege of 1565, thus checking the advance of Suleiman I; and when Lita and I decided to take a swim, we found that to get to the pool we had to walk through a long series of gardens, where beautiful trees shielded us from Malta's "Spanish" sun. So I realized that, like Castile, this is a land grateful for the least watery caress, and quite capable of having been a paradise of trees and flowers, before men started cutting down the forest, some of which still survives on the western side of the island and on Gozo. Here local tradition places Kalypso's cave, out of which some wealthy Roman later made a villa, with running water and a marvelous view of the sea. In any case, the poet tells us that the trees Ulysses later felled to build his boat were long since dead and dry, so that even then the island seems to have been on the way to its present barren condition. And Hermes' description of his long overwater flight to this "remote" island, not far from where Alkinoös will later locate the end of the world, confirms my choice, which coincides with that of many commentators. For if one drifts south from the Strait of Messina under the prevailing northeast *gregale,* one can hardly miss Malta unless the *sirocco* strikes, as it did once when I was trying to sail to Syracuse and had to make it with a broken rudder after being blown onto the huge tuna nets that abound in these waters.

And there are two more coincidences in favor of Malta: first that St. Paul was also shipwrecked there in A.D. 60, "and received no little kindness,"[2] though probably not of the sort dispensed by Kalypso; and second that Kalypso was the daughter of Atlas, and therefore well placed between Europe and Africa, and likely to recommend, as she later does, her sisters, the Pleiades, as guides.

Kalypso receives Hermes with ambrosia and red nectar, but also with the strong suspicion, soon justified, that the jealous gods will not let her keep her lover, even though she has offered to make him her "lawful consort," a rather high-handed offer from Penelope's point of view. But the beautiful Kalypso is a lonely goddess, for Ulysses tells us that no god or man usually came near her. With a final protest, and after a last night of love, she agrees to let him go, and Ulysses is soon "wielding the double-bladed axe with its handle of olive-wood, and the adze of polished bronze to build a big boat with a deck high enough to carry him across the misty seas."

Twenty trees in all he felled, and lopped their branches with his axe; then trimmed them in a workmanlike manner and trued them to the line. Presently Calypso brought him augers. With these he drilled through all his planks, cut them to fit across each other, and fixed this flooring together by means of dowels driven through the interlocking joints, giving the same width to his boat as a skilled shipwright would choose in designing the hull for a broad-bottomed trading vessel. He next put up the decking, which he fitted to ribs at short intervals, finishing off with long gunwales down the sides. He made a mast to go in the boat, with a yard fitted to it; and a steering-oar too, to keep her on her course. And from stem to stern he fenced her sides with plaited osier twigs and a plentiful backing of brushwood, as some protection against the heavy seas. Meanwhile the goddess Calypso had brought him cloth with which to make the sail. This he manufactured too; and then lashed the braces, halyards, and sheets in their places on board. Finally he dragged her down on rollers into the tranquil sea.

By the end of the fourth day all his work was done, and on the fifth beautiful Calypso saw him off from the island. The goddess had bathed him first

2. Acts 28:2.

and fitted him out with fragrant clothing. She had also stowed two skins in his boat, one full of dark wine, the other and larger one of water, besides a leather sack of corn and quantities of appetizing meats And now a warm and gentle breeze sprang up at her command.[iv]

Before tracing Ulysses' next journey, I must pause to consider this description of his boat, which has traditionally been imagined as a raft, while to me its construction corresponds rather to that of a sailboat. This idea has lately received support from the description of the Mycenaean trading ship found at Cape Gelydonia in southern Turkey by Peter Throckmorton. As George T. Bass has pointed out, even the "plaited osier twigs and plentiful backing of brushwood" were actually found at Gelydonia, and it seems clear that they were used to protect the passengers and cargo from the hard gunwales in heavy seas, a precaution that might well be necessary in a boat but certainly not on a raft. Of course I would expect Ulysses' boat to be smaller than the wreck at Gelydonia, which is eight or nine meters long. With the raft in mind, Ulysses' lone journey has been compared with Heyerdahl's crossing of the Pacific; but for those who want a modern counterpart I recommend Joshua Slocum,[3] who at the end of the nineteenth century was the first to sail alone around the world, in *Spray*, a simple sloop with a jigger mast that could be stepped aft of her wheel.

And here are Zeus's plans for this leg of Ulysses' homecoming:

He shall make it in hardship, in a boat put together by his own hands; and on the twentieth day he should reach Scherie, the rich country of the Phaeacians, our kinsmen, who will take him to their hearts and treat him like a god. They will convey him by ship to his own land, giving him copper, gold, and woven materials in such quantities as he could never have won for himself from Troy. . . .[v]

It was with a happy heart that the good Odysseus spread his sail to catch the wind and used his seamanship to keep his boat straight with the steering-

3. See Bibliography.

oar. There he sat and never closed his eyes in sleep, but kept them on the Pleiads, or watched Bootes slowly set, or the Great Bear, nicknamed the Wain, which always wheels round in the same place and looks across at Orion the Hunter with a wary eye. It was this constellation, the only one which never bathes in Ocean's Stream, that the wise goddess Calypso had told to keep on his left hand as he made across the sea. So for seventeen days he sailed on his course, and on the eighteenth there hove into sight the shadowy mountains of the Phaeacians' country, which jutted out to meet him there. The land looked like a shield laid on the misty sea.[vi]

In these two quotations, and in *The Odyssey*'s other descriptions of the Phaiakians' land to which I will refer later, we find all the following elements to pin down this leg of the Odyssey, as well as the basis for my chapter on Ulysses' stars, which point to the bard's home.

1. *Duration.* Eighteen days and nights, once more a magic multiple of 9, but as long as any in the whole voyage. And since in this case we have both a good boat and a willing helmsman sailing a straight course day and night before a godsent wind, the distance covered must be the greatest in *The Odyssey*. And we know that Ulysses sailed night and day because he had to use the stars to navigate.

2. *Direction.* The stars mentioned leave no doubt that Ulysses must have sailed due east, aided by Kalypso's warm wind and by the current that to this day runs counterclockwise around the eastern Mediterranean, and therefore from Malta, south of Crete, toward Cyprus. It is interesting to note that we still use the phrase "to be oriented by the stars," which may commemorate this earliest recorded instance of their being used to sail precisely toward the Orient.

3. *Destination.* A land whose people are human enough to sail instead of flying like Hermes, but remote enough to be singled out by Zeus himself as his kinsmen whose magic ships need no steering oar,[vii] and practical enough to give Ulysses that of which they have the most: copper, the metal that took its name from remote yet Greek Cyprus, the

metal that the wreck at Gelydonia was carrying from Cyprus, and the metal that Athena, in the form of Taphian Mentes, went to buy with iron at Tamesa, Cyprian Tamassos.[viii]

Several more reasons for my choice will be given later, but for the present I feel that these suffice to reject the traditional location of Scheria on Corcyra, or Corfu, sixty miles north of Ithaka, and therefore hardly "remote." Not without regret, however, for Corfu's gentle beauty would have made an ideal frame for Navsikaa, the only woman in *The Odyssey* who managed to steal a corner of Ulysses' heart, and also of mine. But the realities of the sea must rule this search of ours, and had Ulysses sailed from Malta to Corfu, he would certainly have followed the "sole" of the Italian "boot," rather than embark on the loneliest of all his passages, with only the stars for company. Even modern sailing directions recommend the coastal route to Corfu for yachts, and anyhow the Great Bear would have been well ahead of Ulysses' left (fine on the port beam) had he sailed to Corfu.

Nevertheless, I did undertake to study the classic idea that Ulysses ended his voyage sailing into the Adriatic, when I flew in a borrowed Beechcraft all the way down the beautiful Yugoslavian coast, leading a squadron from the Fédération Aéronautique Internationale, which disintegrated almost as quickly as Ulysses'. One carefree Englishman flew low over a pretty island, was forced down by fighters, and ended up visiting Marshal Tito. Later, another member of our squadron, a Frenchman, had to land on a Bulgarian farm, where all went well, according to him, "except for the food." And I had to talk my way out of half a dozen official receptions in as many "satellite" countries.

Nor did Corcyra let us steal away her legend without one last temptation: one of those days in late fall when the gods of sea and air hold their breath in envy of Earth's untimely smile. Rocks and trees seem cut out of the light-blue sky by the sun's already silver shears; and the dappled waters, freezing green below, barely whisper to the beach. A man's heart hums quietly to itself as if it knew neither love nor death, and his eyes adjust to the perfect light of things as they must have been created . . . until a fat sea gull dares to laugh out loud, and breaks the spell. No, Navsikaa is not Corcyra's.

As for Ulysses' landfall, the gods are not through with him yet. His old enemy Poseidon, who was away in Ethiopia when Zeus decided to allow Ulysses' homecoming, spots him from the mountains of the Solymoi, just as Ulysses comes within sight of Scheria, land of the Phaiakians. And Selimiye is in southern Turkey, which, if the coincidence means anything, places the god in the right place to spy his victim coming up on Cyprus (and not on Corfu). Though Poseidon knows he cannot thwart the will of his brother Zeus, he decides to send Ulysses a last "bellyful of trouble" and works up a storm in which all four winds vie in the darkness, sending Ulysses overboard and destroying his boat. For two nights and days he is lost in the heavy seas, protected only by the magic veil given him by "Ino of the slim ankles," latest of his unfailing line of female rescuers, until "Athena, daughter of Zeus, decided to intervene. She roused up the swift North Wind, and stilled all the other winds, and beat the waves down in Ulysses' path, so that he might land among the sea-faring Phaiakians." [ix]

Thus I knew that Ulysses must have approached the coast from the north, and its exact description comes next in *The Odyssey:*

When he had come within call of the shore, he heard the thunder of surf on a rocky coast. With an angry roar the great seas were battering at the ironbound land and all was veiled in spray. There were no coves, no harbours that would hold a ship; nothing but headlands jutting out, sheer rock, and jagged reefs. . . .

Deep water [was] near in; and never a spot where a man could stand on both his feet. . . .

Getting clear of the coastal breakers as he struggled to the surface, he now swam along outside them, keeping an eye on the land, in the hope of lighting on some natural harbour with shelving beaches. Presently his progress brought him off the mouth of a fast-running stream, and it struck him that this was the best spot he could find, for it was not only clear of rocks but sheltered from the winds. . . .

He found a copse with a clear space all round it. Here he crept under a pair of bushes, one an olive, the other a wild olive, which grew from the same stem.[4] . . . He set to work with his hands and scraped up a roomy couch. . . . And now Athene filled Odysseus's eyes with sleep and sealed their lids—the surest way to relieve the exhaustion caused by so much toil.[x]

To locate this landfall, Lita and I flew to Cyprus in a single-engined Cessna owned by Maurice Baird-Smith, who met us at Smyrna with his beautiful wife, Monique, an amateur parachutist who fortunately did not find occasion to practice her favorite sport during this trip. Earlier, in Istanbul, Lita and I had haggled for trinkets over a cup of tea at the Great Bazaar, and browsed through Topkapi, the pleasantest of museums, noting once again that our world is as varied as that of *The Odyssey*. Now the four of us enjoyed the view from the air of the marvelous Ionian coast as we flew low to the south over the straits of Chios, Kolophon, Ephesos, the Maeander River, Miletos, and Halicarnassos. Then we turned east along ancient Lycia, where the Mycenaean wreck lies off Gelydonia, a coast whose beauty is still unspoiled though it faces the sun, which in the Mediterranean usually brings buses and hotels. Finally we flew high across the water to drop down on Cape Arnauti, the northwestern corner of Cyprus, where I think Ulysses must have made his landfall, near where Venus bathed at Fontana Amorosa. And as I watched the rugged Cyprian coast unfold to the south, down to the river mouth near Paphos where Aphrodite was born, I saw, superimposed like a three-thousand-year double exposure on Homer's description of Ulysses' landing, our modern *Sailing Directions for the Mediterranean:* "Nearshore approaches to Cyprus are encumbered by above- and below-water rocks, and the 6 fathom curve lies within one mile of shore. Be-

4. Exactly what happens to our olive trees in Cadaqués if they are not properly looked after, which is usually the case.

tween Cape Arnauti and Paphos Point, about 22 miles south-southeast-
ward, the intervening coast has islets, reefs and ledges close off shore on
which the sea breaks almost constantly." [5]

Satisfied, we landed at Nicosia, and spent the next few days exploring
the island by land and by air with Desmond Watkins and his air-minded
wife, who live in Cyprus. No one bothered us as our plane shuttled in
and out of the airport, though we did once pick up ice in a cloud, which
is nasty and unexpected at these latitudes. On land the frequent Turkish
and Greek roadblocks always seemed to open before Watkins' British
papers, but after we left, Maurice Baird-Smith forwarded to us the following note, which proved once more that enmity between Trojans and
Greeks is not yet dead: "You might be interested and amused to know that
our aerial trip nearly caused an international incident. It seems we flew
over forbidden Turkish and Greek strongholds from directions which
made the Greeks think we were Turks and the Turks Greeks. We were the
subject of official complaints, and the Turks accused everyone of spying
and aerial photography and have said they will 'shoot down all future
transgressors.' No one, however, knows (or admits) that it was us. The
control tower denied all knowledge, and United Nations investigation
failed to reveal anything at all about the plane or its source! So much for
the U.N. In fact, our photography may reveal hidden secrets but, hope-
fully, only about Ulysses."

NAVSIKAA'S SCHERIA
(Cyprus)

Young Navsikaa of the white arms, tall and beautiful as a goddess . . .

"Never yet have my eyes beheld such a mortal, whether man or
woman. Amazement holds me as I look. Only in Delos have I seen the like,

5. U.S.H.O. 55, 5-3, 5A-1.

a fresh young palm-tree by the altar of Apollo." [xi] Thus does Ulysses address the daughter of King Alkinoös of Scheria when, after sleeping exhausted through almost twenty-four hours, he is awakened in the afternoon by Navsikaa's happy cries as she plays with her maidens by the mouth of the river. Ulysses has emerged "like a mountain lion from beneath the bushes, his head and shoulders still befouled with brine and hiding his nakedness with a leafy bough" [xii] and has asked for hospitality. Understandably, Navsikaa's maidens have fled, but the princess has stood firm and now takes pity on the fearsome stranger in whom she sees the victim of Olympian Zeus, "who as it pleases him dispenses happiness to each man, whether good or evil." [xiii]

She arranges for him to be bathed, anointed, and dressed; and Athena, who inspired Navsikaa in the first place to go to the river to wash the palace's stored clothes near where Ulysses slept, now intervenes to transform her favorite into a demigod, so that Navsikaa cannot help saying: "If only such a man might settle here and be my husband. . . . But come, stranger, that I may escort you to my father's house. Walk quickly with my handmaids behind the mules and the waggon, but when we reach a goodly grove of poplar trees, sacred to Athena, sit down there, and wait until we reach the city and my father's house. Otherwise, some base fellow might say, 'Who is this tall, handsome stranger following Navsikaa? Doubtless a husband for her, since she scorns her countrymen here, although she has many noble suitors.' But when you have entered the palace, pass by my father, and embrace my mother's knees, where she sits spinning the purple yarn in the light of the fire. If you gain her favor, you can hope to receive help in returning home." [xiv]

Ingenuous wisdom as well as beauty, and in a flash Ulysses knows the princess's feelings, and how she wishes him to behave; but his own feelings, though they have withstood the love of more than one goddess, will give him more trouble as he walks through the sunny island that Navsikaa has described: "We dwell far off in the surging sea, and are the furthermost of mortals. Around our city runs a high wall, and we have a fair harbor on either side, with a narrow causeway leading to it. Each man has his own station for his own ship, and the curved ships are drawn up along the road. Here the people assemble around the fair temple of Poseidon, its huge stones sunk deep in the earth, and the men attend to the tackle of their black ships, the cables and sails, and shape the thin blades of their oars." [xv] And the poet adds that Alkinoös' orchard produces "pear, pomegranate, apple, sweet fig, and luxuriant olive. And there is never a time when the West Wind's breath is not quickening some fruits to life and ripening others. There too is his fruitful vineyard." [xvi] Now Cyprus, apart from copper, is famous for wine and fruit, and the sailing directions say that on all coasts of Cyprus a west wind is prevalent in summer, and frequent in winter. So that our identification continued to grow on us as we photographed a double harbor [6] still visible near Paphos, not far from a banana plantation which would surely have pleased Alkinoös, or from Maa, where many of the objects I will mention in Chapter V were found.

Ulysses crosses the threshold of Alkinoös' splendid dwelling and enters the court, whose walls of bronze are topped with blue enamel tiles. He passes through golden doors hung on posts of silver and flanked by gold and silver dogs made by Hephaistos himself. Inside the hall, lighted by flaming torches held by golden figures of youths, the king sits in counsel with the Phaiakian sea lords, all on high chairs ranged along the walls and covered with delicately woven cloth. Protected by a magic mist sent by Athena, the suppliant reaches Arete, the queen, and as soon as he has made his plea, the mist disperses and Alkinoös and his nobles vote to convey Ulysses to his home. But quick-eyed Arete (whose name means "unity of mind and body," something very dear to the Greeks) has recognized Ulysses' borrowed cloak as one she herself wove with her maids. For she heads a household of fifty, "some to grind the yellow corn, some

6. See photo page 145.

Navsikaa's Scheria, near Paphos

to weave cloth or twirl the yarn, their hands busily rustling like the tall poplar's leaves, while the soft olive-oil drips from the closely woven linen." [xvii] So it is the queen who begins to interrogate Ulysses, and in the ensuing conversation a charming portrait emerges of Mycenaean frankness and tact.

As Ulysses tells how he has found his way to Alkinoös' palace, the king exclaims that his daughter did wrong in not bringing Ulysses directly home. Ulysses does not give the true explanation (Navsikaa's prudent fear of showing her sudden love for him in public) but rather takes the responsibility upon himself, explaining that he was afraid that Alkinoös might not have liked to see a stranger arrive with his daughter, "for we men are jealous folk." Far from accepting this easy explanation, Alkinoös betrays his knowledge of Navsikaa's motives and feelings: "I could wish for nothing better than that so goodly a man, and one so like-minded with me, would become husband to my daughter and take his place as my son and live here in a house I would give him and furnish for him. But if you wish to go, not one of us Phaiakians will keep you against your will."

The king says something else, the geographic implications of which bothered me considerably, as they have bothered some of my predecessors: he brags that his sailors have even gone as far as Euboia, "which is said to be the farthest land," a confusing statement if we consider that the well-known island of Euboia brackets half the eastern coast of Greece, within the relatively cozy Aegean. This neighborly "farthest land" seemed to defy explanation until by chance, while studying the ancient *Periplus* of Scylax, I spotted an island that he places between Sardinia and Tunis, just about where in my view Ulysses made the almost fatal move west and into the hands of the Cyclops. This island, today called La Galite, clearly marks the farthest end of the eastern Mediterranean and Tyrrhenian as viewed from Cyprus; beyond it the sea opens wide into the western Mediterranean. To a Cypriot sailor this could certainly be the farthest land, and Scylax gives us the island's name: Euboia Insula.[7] So here is one more example of how migrant Greeks took their place names with them, for the first Greek colonists in the West, the founders of Cumae and Pithekoussai, came from Chalcis in Aegean Euboia.

The conversation over, Arete invites Ulysses to dine and then to rest in the echoing portico, just as Nestor is inviting Telemachos at just about the same moment in time, as told at the beginning of *The Odyssey*. And the poet adds: "Then Ulysses realized how welcome it would be to lie down to sleep." [xviii]

Next day, at the assembly, Alkinoös presents his guest to his captains and counselors. "I do not know his name," he says, reminding us that it is impolite to ask a guest his name before he has rested, dined, and been entertained, "nor whether he journeys from Eastern or from Western lands," [xix] a clear reference to Cyprus's position as maritime crossroad between East and West, between Greece's own Europe and her ancient and long-lasting enemy, Asia. And having agreed to man a ship with fifty-two noble young oarsmen, the "sceptered kings" of Phaiakia repair to Alkinoös' palace to feast, to listen to blind Demodokos, the bard who has often been accepted as a self-portrait of Homer, and to hear the rest of Ulysses' story—another picture typical of the feudal world I have described, and one more detail to liken Phaiakia to Cyprus, known in the ancient world as an island of kings who sometimes made their peace with Persia, sometimes with Greece.

Demodokos sings of the quarrel of Ulysses and Achilles at Troy, "a story well-known by then throughout the world," which fits well with the tradition that Paphos was founded by Agapenor, the Arcadian king who fought at Troy, while Cypriot Salamis was founded by Teucer, brother of Ajax and son of Telamon, king of Attic Salamis and another hero of the Siege. Remembering Troy, Ulysses hides his tears under his cloak

---

7. Nordenskiöld (see Bibliography).

and behind his two-handled cup, but not from the king, who sits next to him and who, with characteristic tact, proposes to move outdoors to the games, where "the Phaiakian nobles have gone to watch boxing, wrestling, jumping and foot-races."[xx]

Things take a nasty turn when young Euryalos, trying to needle the reluctant Ulysses into competing, compares him to "some old skipper of a merchant ship, who spends his life on a hulking tramp, worrying about his freight and keeping a sharp eye on the cargo he is bringing home and the profit he is greedy for," a feudal lord's view of trade, which is best left to others. But nimble-witted Ulysses reacts in style by pointing out that Euryalos can hardly have brains as well as such good looks, and by picking up the biggest stone disk of all and sending it humming beyond all the Phaiakians' efforts. Then, emboldened by his success, he proceeds to brag of his prowess in sport, and to challenge any Phaiakian at any sport, "except my host, for the man who challenges his host endangers his own prospects."

But tactful Alkinoös intervenes once more, calling for the dance that is an integral part of the games, and pointing out that the Phaiakians, though first-rate seamen and sportsmen, still delight most in the gentler gifts of civilization: "the banquet, the lyre, the dance, clean linen, warm baths, and our beds," [xxi] a good list of Mediterranean luxuries. At the king's words, "the committee of nine official stewards elected to supervise such occasions" [xxii] sends for Demodokos, who now administers a gentle rebuke to young Euryalos by singing of old Hephaistos' vengeance on his rival, Ares. And his song ends significantly for our identification, with the arrival of "laughter-loving Aphrodite at Paphos in Cyprus." Finally, at Alkinoös' suggestion, the twelve princes of the island fill a coffer provided by Arete with gifts of "indestructible copper," of clothing and of gold, as well as bronze three-legged caldrons such as the one Arete's maids have used to heat Ulysses' bath. Even impertinent Euryalos, repentant, presents Ulysses with a sword of bronze with a silver hilt and a sheath of fresh ivory. Alkinoös tops off the gifts with a golden chalice, and reassures the nobles that their generous expenses will easily be recouped by a special tax on the people, which makes him as modern a ruler as any. The company assembles once again to hear Demodokos sing, at Ulysses' request, of the wooden horse of Troy, a story that Ulysses cannot stand without again breaking into tears, and this finally brings the tactful Phaiakian king to ask him point-blank for his name and his story, which Ulysses proceeds to tell at length.

Then Ulysses meets Navsikaa for the last time, in all her "heaven-sent beauty, standing by one of the pillars that support the massive roof." "Farewell, my friend," she says, "and hereafter, even in your native land, I hope that you will remember me." To which Ulysses replies: "If Zeus, Hera's loud-thundering lord, grants that I may reach my home, I will worship you all the rest of my days. For it was you, lady, who saved me." [xxiii] So few are the words Homer needs to close this gentle story of love and fate.

The last tear shed, Ulysses cannot wait to be off at dusk, and after a special toast to the queen his protector, he boards the Phaiakians' black ship. Alkinoös has said: "Our ships understand on their own the intentions of their crew, and find their way without pilots or steering-oars such as other ships require." [xxiv] Is Alkinoös' claim simply a seaman's exaggeration, or were the Phaiakians the first to use an automatic pilot such as often freed my hands in *Oh Papa* to navigate, take notes, and direct Lita's photography? When I had been considering the possibility of Ulysses' having sailed north after Gibraltar, I toyed with the idea that if Scheria was to be found in northern Europe, the Phaiakians might have brought Ulysses back to the Mediterranean by floating him down the Rhine and the Rhône, just as Marinatos thinks the amber found in the tombs of royal Mycenaeans came down the rivers from the North Sea.[8] But, though this might have explained the ship's homing instinct, my theory soon went the way of so many others that I tried and rejected

8. See Bibliography.

without further mention. Cousin Raf, whom I mentioned in my Prologue, says that a modern or even a lateen rig would permit sailing across a steady *meltemi* from Cyprus to Greece and back with a fixed tiller, which makes me think that perhaps the Phaiakians' magic lay simply in having invented (or introduced to the Greek world) the lateen sail. But again, I hesitate to make the affirmation unless or until the archaeologists come up with a contemporary Cypriot model or drawing of a lateener. The closest I have been able to come to such a drawing is the painting on the north wall of the tomb of Asa, at Deir el Gebrâwi in Egypt (about 2170 B.C.), which shows two triangular sails not unlike lateeners.[9] If they are indeed lateeners, they would set the origin of these sails at least two thousand years before the date now generally accepted. Slocum, by the way, sailed twenty-seven hundred miles from Thursday Island to the Keeling Cocos in twenty-three days, with the tiller lashed all the time except for one hour.

The Phaiakians "untie the cable from the pierced stone," identical to the many Mycenaean anchors found by modern archaeologists, and the magic ship heads for Ithaka so fast that a great wave forms in her wake, just as it does behind a modern speedboat. "As a team of four stallions yoked abreast rears and plunges as one horse, the ship lunged forward, and her stern began to rise and fall above the great dark wave that the sea sent roaring in her wake. As she sped forward, not even the wheeling hawk, the fastest thing that flies, could have kept pace. And when the most brilliant star rose, that harbinger of the tender light of dawn, the ship drew near to Ithaka."[xxv] This has given rise to the supposition that Ulysses reached Ithaka from Scheria in one night, impossible if we place Scheria in Cyprus, but I believe that there is no problem here but rather a choice. Homer says that Ulysses set out at sunset and landed at dawn, but he does not say that it was the next dawn, so that we may, if we wish, understand that more than one day

9. N. de G. Davies, thanks to Dr. Kent R. Weeks of the Metropolitan Museum of Art, New York City (see Bibliography).

has passed during Ulysses' magic sleep, "most sweet and profound, in semblance much like death," [xxvi] from which he is not awakened even when the ship is beached at full speed. Or we can accept the explanation that Homer seems at such pains to emphasize: that everything in this trip is magic, which indicates that even the bard himself felt that the final leg of Ulysses' voyage was so long that it needed more than a natural explanation. This would support my choice of Cyprus, the easternmost extreme of the Greek-speaking world, a choice consistent with Homer's fond telling of the whole Phaiakian episode, if, as I shall show, the stars place the poet's home on Cyprus. And one more coincidence is worth noting: the Phaiakians claim to have migrated from Hyperia, to escape the Cyclopes, and their use of sea-purple as a dye is mentioned twice. Now the Phoenicians are supposed to have brought sea-purple from the Balearics, and thus the history of the Phaiakians closely parallels Ulysses' journey home from the land of the Cyclopes, on Minorca, via Sicily, the land of Hyperion, the Sun God.

In any case the gods must have the last word in this story, and Poseidon, after asking permission of Zeus, will have his. Once the Phaiakians have deposited Ulysses and his treasure in Phorkys' Cove on Ithaka, they head for home; and as they come into sight of Scheria, and Alkinoös prepares to welcome them, he sees his father's ancient prophecy come true: "Poseidon struck the ship with one blow of the flat of his hand and turned the ship to stone, rooted on the bottom of the sea." [xvii]

This ship of stone must be one of the many islets that dot the eastern shore of Cyprus, such as Orphourous, whose name bears memories of dark magic and of ships, for Orpheus was a famous Thracian poet who became an Argonaut and was torn to pieces by the Bacchantes. Thus does Ulysses finally escape his fate, but at the price set by the gods, who can never let mortals forget them, for fear of ceasing to exist.

ITHAKA

(*still Ithaka*)

As *Oh Papa* droned toward the Ionian islands of Zakynthos, Cephalonia, and Ithaka, I reviewed in my mind the old arguments about Ulysses' kingdom caused by the two Homeric descriptions that should by all accounts be the most reliable and that, unaccountably, appear to be the only ones in *The Odyssey* quite incompatible with geography.

When Menelaos offers young Telemachos three horses as a gift, Ulysses' son is quite definite: "Horses I will not take to Ithaka, where there are no wide courses for them, nor any meadowland, for it is a pasture land for goats," [xxviii] a description that is later confirmed by Athena herself. And, awaiting Telemachos' return to his capital, the suitors set their ambush for him "out in the open sea, midway between Ithaka and rugged Samos, where the rocky isle of Asteris, small as it is, has a harbour with two mouths." [xxix] So far so good.

But Ulysses, when he finally tells his story to the Phaiakians at Alkinoös' request, adds information as to Ithaka's relative position that cannot be ignored: "I am Ulysses, Laertes' son. I dwell in clearly seen Ithaka, whereon is the wooded peak of Neriton. For neighbors we have many peopled isles close together, Doulichion and Samos and wooded Zakynthos. But Ithaka, the farthest out to sea, lies slanting to the west, whereas the others face the dawn. It is a rugged island, but a good nurse for young men." [xxx]

Now, modern Ithaka is certainly no place for horses, as Lita's photograph clearly shows.[10] On it stands Mount Neriton, and in the channel that separates it from Cephalonia, whose capital still bears the name of

10. See photo page 153.

Ithaka

Samos, lies the island of Deskalio, from which the suitors could well have watched for Telemachos to sail up the Ithaka channel to his capital, which I place near Polis Bay. But by no stretch of the imagination can we say with Ulysses that modern Ithaka is the farthest of the islands out to sea and lies slanting to the west, whereas the others face the dawn.[11] This is perhaps the toughest geographic problem in the whole of *The Odyssey* and has given rise to any number of theories, none of which is quite satisfactory, though some experts, like Schliemann's partner Dörpfeld, have gone so far as to place ancient Ithaka on Levkas, switching the names of the other islands, while others have preferred Cephalonia because it really does lie to the west.

As I watched from the sky, I tried two new theories: could the western part of Cephalonia originally have been separated from the rest of the island, to which it is now joined by a low isthmus? This could certainly have created an Ithaka out to sea and to the west. Or could the dramatic peninsula of Assos, joined as it is today to the western coast of Cephalonia by the narrowest spit of land, have been the site of Ulysses' palace? From the air it looks like a perfect citadel, reminiscent of French Mont-Saint-Michel, and strewn with ruins to boot; and Herodotos, "the father of history," tells us that the sea used to wash over the neck that joins Assos to Cephalonia. But after months of studying the evidence I came to the simplest conclusion: Ithaka is Ithaka and has borne that name at least since classical times, coins from which have been found on the island; and Ulysses' palace will be found on the northern end of the island, not far from Polis, which must have been its port, hard by Deskalio, the only Asteris available for the suitors' trap. What Ulysses meant when he said that Ithaka was the farthest out to sea of the four islands, I frankly do not know. But to this day the three islands do carry names clearly reminiscent of Ulysses' list, and the fourth, Doulichion, must be the peninsula of Levkas, right next to which lies Meganisi, whose

11. See chart page 35.

name reminds us of Meges, to whom the Homeric Catalogue of Ships assigns Doulichion. All other solutions would oblige us to abandon an Ithaka unfit for horses, and worse still leave us without Asteris, where the suitors laid their trap, both items more important to Homer's narrative than the western position of Ithaka. If one cannot find a perfect theory, one must choose the one that gives least trouble, unlike some theorists whose desperation drives them to ever more complicated propositions.

So the Phaiakians land the sleeping Ulysses on today's Ithaka "after beaching their ship up to half her length at an inlet named after Phorkys, the Old Man of the Sea, where two sheer headlands screen the harbor from the great breakers. At the head of the cove grows a long-leaved olive tree, and near it is a cavern inhabited by Nymphs in which the honey bees hive; it has two mouths, one facing north and the second south; this, being meant for the gods, is never used by men." [xxxi] Ulysses awakes on the beach and fails to recognize his long-lost homeland because Athena has thrown her magic mist about the place in order to gain time to disguise herself as a young man, appear to Ulysses, and make plans for his return to the palace. But Ulysses instinctively invents a story for the "young man," arousing the mirth of the goddess, who reveals herself to him without further attempt at deceiving the arch-deceiver. "Who can keep up with your craftiness?" she cries. "That is why I have not despaired for you: you are so civil, so intelligent, so shrewd," [xxxii] a perfect description of the Mycenaean ideal, a man of whom no one can make a fool, an ideal that seems to me to survive today among Latins and Slavs, while Anglo-Saxons (honestly or not) tend to emphasize honesty rather than cleverness.

Yet the story Ulysses invents for the ears of a stranger, who may well have seen the Phaiakian ship bring him in and put to sea again, contains a piece of information that supports my location of Scheria on Cyprus rather than on Corfu: Ulysses claims that the ship, after putting him ashore, set sail for "the fine city of Sidon," very much in the same direction as Cyprus from Ithaca, and not at all in the direction of Corfu.

Ulysses and Athena hide his treasure in the cave, their attitude similar to our Venetian friend's, who enjoined us to lock up our cameras, saying: "Here everyone is quite honest, but things are always missing!" Then Athena transforms her ward into a balding beggar, and bids him seek out old Eumaios, the loyal swineherd, "near the Raven's Crag and the fountain of Arethusa"; [xxxiii] while she herself goes to Sparta to summon Telemachos, who is even now consulting Menelaos. So the poet's story comes full circle, for this is where *The Odyssey* began.

But I must still identify the Cove of Phorkys and its Cave of the Nymphs, and after checking all the proposals of which I have notice, I have reached the conclusion that the cove is that of Polis, where I have situated the port of Ulysses' capital.[12] Other commentators, though not all, have accepted Polis for Ithaka's main port, but have suggested different landing places for Ulysses' return, mostly in the south of the island. I think it makes most sense that the godlike Phaiakians should deposit Ulysses at his home port, since the suitors are waiting on Asteris-Deskalio only for Telemachos, and will surely not give away their intentions by boarding any other ship. And on the northwest side of Polis Bay there is just the cave we need, where excavations carried out in the thirties by Miss Benton of the British School in Athens uncovered inscriptions referring to the nymphs, to Athena, and to Ulysses himself—and, best of all, twelve bronze tripod-caldrons such as Ulysses received from the twelve kings of Scheria.[13] Much of what was found dated from the late Bronze Age, and the caldrons, though more recent, certainly antedate *The Odyssey* itself, and could at least have given rise to the tradition Homer used for the details of his story. Miss Benton also uncovered a Mycenaean site at Tris Langadas on the northern slope of Polis valley, and though through the years it has been greatly disturbed

12. See chart page 35.
13. Reports 35, 39, and 42, B.S.A.

by terracing for vineyards so that no complete plan has yet emerged, this could well have been Ulysses' palace.[14]

As for Telemachos, Athena finds him lying awake in Menelaos' portico, and forthwith sends him home, after warning him of the suitors' ambush. "Give those islands a wide berth and sail both day and night. Land on the nearest point in Ithaka and send the ship and the whole ship's company round to the city; then you head straight off to visit your swineherd, who is loyal to you." [xxxiv] So, the stage is set for the final act, and from Athena's words it seems logical that Telemachos will sail up the coast of Elis, west of the Echinades, and then south of Arkudi into Phrikes Bay, whence he can make his way to Eumaios' hut from the eastern shore of Ithaka, while Ulysses approaches from the western shore "over a rough path climbing up from the woods into the highlands." [xxxv] This places the Raven's Crag (Korax) and the fountain of Arethusa somewhere near Kalamos, where local tradition will have it, and near where Mycenaean sherds have been found at Ayios Athanasios. And, having escaped the suitors, Telemachos sends his ship "round" the north end of Ithaka to "the port," Polis.

Meanwhile Ulysses, in beggar's guise, enjoys the hospitality of Eumaios, the faithful but pessimistic swineherd, who is sure that Ulysses the king is dead, yet keeps on doing his best to tend the king's herds of six hundred cows and three hundred and sixty white-tusked boars, despite the demands of the suitors who "at regular intervals order him to send down the pick of his fatted hogs for their banquets." Eumaios completes the picture of Ulysses' wealth by adding that the long-lost king owned "on the mainland, twelve droves of cattle, twelve flocks of sheep, twelve herds of pigs, and twelve troops of goats; and in Ithaka eleven troops of goats." [xxxvi] Which confirms once more that Ithaka has little pasture for horses or for cattle but only for goats and hogs, as does the fact that Noëmon, whose ship Telemachos borrows, soon becomes impatient be-

14. Reports 40 and 41, B.S.A.

cause he wants to sail to mainland Elis where he keeps his horses and mules.[xxxvii] And Eurymachos' statement that the cattle on the mainland are "tended by hired men as well as by the King's own herdsmen" confirms the impression given also by *The Iliad*'s Catalogue of Ships, that Ulysses is king only of the "Cephalenes" who people three islands: Cephalonia, which being the biggest and most populous has given the people their name; Ithaka, which being the easiest to defend contains the citadel or capital; and wooded Zakynthos to the south. Doulichion forms part of the mainland kingdom of Meges, from whom Ulysses probably leases land for his cattle.

For Eumaios, Ulysses the beggar spins yet another tale to explain how he knows that Ulysses the king is about to return "between the waning of the old moon and the waxing of the new." He claims to be the last son of Castor the Cretan and to have followed King Idomeneus of Crete to Troy. There he supposedly took part in one raid as "third in command" after Menelaos and Ulysses, whose famous cunning he says he knows at first hand. After Troy he claims to have sailed from Crete to Egypt in five days with a fresh and favorable wind from the north, and thence to Phoenicia. Then on his way to Libya he says he was wrecked southwest of Crete, and drifted to Thesprotia coiled around the mast of the wrecked ship. In Thesprotia, in northwest Greece where modern Ioannina lies, King Pheidon has given him news of Ulysses the king, who has gone to Dodona to consult the oracle before being conveyed home. Then Pheidon has sent "the Cretan" to Doulichion, the corn island, but the crew has plotted to reduce their passenger to slavery, so that he is forced to swim ashore on Ithaka, where it must be assumed they planned to sell their new slave on their way round the south of Levkas and toward Meganisi or Nidri, on Levkas' east coast, which may have been the capital of Doulichion.[15]

This tale so intrigued me at first that I even considered the possibility

15. See chart page 35.

that it might contain the true itinerary of *The Odyssey*, the one told to
the Phaiakians being false. But I came to the conclusion that wily Ulysses was more likely to have told the truth to the kinsmen of the gods,
from whom he needed safe passage, than to the swineherd to whom he
only needed to show that the king was about to return. So the story is
false, but coming from such an accomplished liar, it must be credible,
and its geography must make sense. If I have interpreted it rightly, two
important conclusions are to be drawn: first that Eumaios' hut is in the
north of Ithaka, the only part of the island close to the Thesprotian
ship's course as she sails around Levkas, which confirms my choice of
Polis for Ulysses' real landing place, whence he walked to Eumaios';
and second that my explanation of why Ulysses sailed west along the
coast of Libya when he was blown there from Malea agrees with his
claim of having sailed from Crete to Egypt in five days with a favorable
wind from the north, for he thought he was being blown from Malea to
Egypt in nine days with his sail furled.[16]

Once Ulysses and Telemachos have joined forces, they descend in-
evitably upon the palace, where Ulysses is almost given away by his dog
Argos. But *The Odyssey* must end with justice and with death, meted
out to the greedy suitors by father and son in a joyfully grim ballet whose
choreography (by gray-eyed Athena) welds them at last, after twenty
years, into an invincible team; and anyone who has seen his own experience appreciated and used by his son can well imagine Ulysses' joy.

We have already seen that the west wind dominates the eastern Mediterranean, so that the east wind necessary to bring Ulysses home from
Cyprus blows only exceptionally in fall, and this fits the autumnal scene
of death with which *The Odyssey* is about to end. For years Penelope
has held off the suitors, chieftains of neighboring islands who have occupied her palace to await her choice of a new king. But the latest of her
excuses, that she is weaving a winding sheet for old Laertes, Ulysses'

16. See Chapter II.

father, and cannot marry until it is done, which obliges her to unravel every night what she has woven during the day, has become suspect. So, finally, she has offered to marry the suitor who can string Ulysses' great bow and shoot an arrow through a line of twelve axes planted in the ground "like timbers to hold a ship." This thwarts all the suitors, for only a Mycenaean as widely traveled as Ulysses can be familiar with the composite bow, and know that to string it one must sit, and use one thigh and the other leg. So only Ulysses the beggar performs the feat, and the suitors' long days of feasting and playing draughts and quoits in his palace are over, as Ulysses drops his mask and slaughters them one by one till the court is awash with blood. Then he hangs the maids who have willingly catered to the suitors' pleasures, and forthwith claims his Penelope, whom he still loves best, perhaps because he has put so much effort into returning to her. But the queen still has doubts, and it takes a little while before the royal pair is reunited, and peace eventually descends upon Homer's world.

We of *Oh Papa* have now followed Ulysses home, so that the dramatic details of this last episode are not within the scope of our airborne Odyssey. But if you have stayed with me this far, heed now my plea and read again Homer's chapters XV to XVIII, and enjoy the most vigorously masculine scenario of courage and of blood ever written.

Having extended Ulysses' voyage south of Philenia, west to the Balearics and east to Cyprus, we will take our leave, flying from Corfu to Venice in such foul weather that we never saw Maurice Baird-Smith, who was flying his plane in the same direction and talking to us on the radio. But a stopover in beautiful Venice is never a waste of time, and when the weather improved we were welcomed back to Geneva, *Oh Papa*'s home, by Mont Blanc, on which we had nearly left our bones when our engine quit at the very beginning of our search.

But before we part, I must bequeath to you one more theory, this one designed to wrest from the stars an answer to the ancient Homeric question: Where and when did Homer live and write his eternal song?

THE HOMERIC
QUESTION

Ulysses' Stars and Homer's Cyprus

ULYSSES' STARS AND HOMER'S CYPRUS

Having completed our airborne Odyssey, we are left with the Homeric question, one of the oldest riddles of history. From the very beginning, I have assumed that Homer existed as an individual, and did in fact write *The Iliad* and *The Odyssey* about real people, among them Ulysses. As pointed out in my Prologue, my faith was based on aesthetic considerations: on the way *The Odyssey* is constructed, and the way its hero enters the stage at the most dramatic moment to unfold his tale, after the poet has paved the way with a description of the Mycenaean world and captured our curiosity with the adventures of Telemachos and the drama of the suitors. All of which makes the appearance of Ulysses as striking as the late entrance of the soloist in a well-prepared piano concerto, say Mozart's Twenty-first. And no audience doubts the existence of Mozart, so why doubt that of Homer?

Consequently, for me, the Homeric question can be put quite simply, though it is far from simple to answer: *When and where did Homer write?*

First *when.* According to historians, it must have been before the founding of Naucratis about 620 B.C.,[1] and archaeologists seem to agree more and more that datable objects mentioned in the poems make it probable that they were written after 750 B.C., though nothing absolutely certain is known of Homer's text until Peisistratos standardized it in the sixth century B.C. for the Panathenaic competitions, where it had to be recited without mistakes.[2] After pondering the arguments, I am ready to accept the round date of 700 B.C., give or take a half century. This

1. Rhys Carpenter (see Bibliography).
2. For a detailed discussion of this subject, see also "The Homeric Question" by J. A. Davidson in Wace and Stubbings (see Bibliography).

163

date is not too distant from the ninth century B.C., where Herodotos (writing in the fifth century) placed Homer. So, based on 700 B.C., I will use celestial navigation to attempt an answer to the other part of the question: *where*. And my star diagram shows that fifty years more or less can make no difference to my argument, since they would affect the diagram by less than one degree on the circle of precession.

When Ulysses finally leaves Kalypso and heads for home, the poet tells us the course he has been instructed by the goddess to sail:

There he sat and never closed his eyes in sleep, but kept them on the Pleiads, or watched Bootes slowly set, or the Great Bear, nicknamed the Wain, which always wheels round in the same place and looks across at Orion the Hunter with a wary eye. It was this constellation, the only one which never bathes in Ocean's Stream, that the wise goddess Calypso had told him to keep on his left hand as he made across the sea.[i]

The stars mentioned are exactly the same ones that appear in the Bible's Book of Job, the same ones which Hesiod used to mark the seasons for farmers, and the same ones that can be recognized in Egyptian frescoes and in paintings found in the Megalithic caves of Bretagne and Vendée. And the Big Bear's habits agree with the myth that Hera, Zeus's nasty wife, jealous of his love for the nymph Callisto, transformed her into a bear and condemned her never to bathe again, a cruel punishment for a dainty nymph; so Zeus put Callisto the bear in the heavens to keep her away from Arcturus, who did not know he was her son. Also, the Pleiades and Arcturus, the brightest star in Boötes, were simultaneously visible in 700 B.C. in fall, which supports my suggestion that this was the season of Ulysses' return, as it was the season of his departure from Troy.

The information the poet gives about the stars mentioned by Kalypso is absolutely precise, both for Ulysses and for us. For Ulysses it establishes the heading he has to hold for home, because it tells him on which hand he has to keep the north, about which the Great Bear wheels. For us the quotation contains something just as important, which seems to have been missed by those who have tried before to retrace his Odyssey: it tells us which constellations disappeared below the horizon as they circled about the pole, and which did not—which is tantamount to telling us the latitudes most familiar to the author of *The Odyssey*, since the altitude above the horizon of any given star at its lowest point is an exact measure of the latitude of the observer, the angular distance of that star from the pole being known. It is reasonable to assume that the poet described stars as he saw them in the latitudes most familiar to himself, for it would be too much to suppose that he took into account the fact that stars seem to behave differently in different latitudes and calculated how they would look elsewhere. *So in 700 B.C. and at the latitudes which were most familiar to the poet, the Great Bear, the one that stalks Orion (sometimes also known as the Chariot) was the only constellation which never dipped below the horizon and into the sea.*

My chart[3] shows the stars mentioned by Homer in this, the earliest of all historical instances of the use of celestial navigation; and in the same diagram I have included the best "home stars" which overheaded Ithaka in 700 B.C., to which I have referred in my discussion of "Latitude Sailing" in Chapter III.[4] Now in constructing this chart the first thing I had to take into account was the fact that almost three thousand years ago, the pole was not where it is now, and Polaris was only remotely polar. The Earth, as it careens around the sun, at the same time spinning about its own axis, also "wobbles" slowly like a top, a motion called precession which was discovered by Hiparcos at Rhodes in 150 B.C. In so doing, the Earth's poles describe in the sky circles whose diameter is about a third of that of the globe, and it takes each pole twenty-six thousand years to complete a full circle and return to any given position.

3. See chart page 102.
4. Note that in Chapter III I was speaking of the home stars that Ulysses must have used, whether Homer knew it or not; whereas in this chapter I refer to a definite "star picture" specifically mentioned by the bard.

So, for example, forty-five centuries ago the North Pole was near the star Thuban in the constellation of the Dragon, and all other stars seemed to circle around Thuban as they now appear to circle around Polaris; and fifty-five centuries from now Alderamin, in Cepheus, will take over as approximate center of the apparent motion of the stars. The stars themselves also move very slowly within their constellations, but the only one that has moved more than one degree since the time of Ulysses is Arcturus, which is not critical for my argument, while the components of the Dipper and Etamin in Draco, which *are* critical, have moved only negligible fractions of a degree.

On my chart I have constructed a section of this circle of precession of the pole, and knowing how long it takes the pole to travel the full circle, I have measured off the position of the pole corresponding to the date I have accepted for Homer, 700 B.C., which puts the pole not far from Kochab in the Little Dipper (or Bear). Now since any given star, as seen from any given latitude while it circles around the pole, can dip below the horizon only if its angular distance from the pole is equal to the latitude of the observer, I have further drawn three circles centered on this ancient pole, which I will call my "horizon circles of latitude." At the latitude corresponding to the diameter of the circle, those stars that remain within the horizon circle of latitude never dipped below the horizon in 700 B.C., whereas those that are left outside the circle invariably did so once every night. And since the poet tells us that the Big Dipper (or Bear) was the only constellation that did not dip, we are obliged to choose a diameter corresponding to a latitude below 37 degrees, for at that latitude, Etamin in Draco also remains above the horizon.

But before stalking closer to my conclusion, I must clear up one problem: it is obvious from my chart that in 700 B.C., regardless of latitude, if the Big Dipper is to be kept dry, the Little Dipper will certainly stay as dry as a bone, which leaves only two alternatives: first, it can be assumed that, since it did not then contain the pole star, the whole of the Little

Dipper must have had little or no importance for Homeric navigators, so that they did not consider it a full-fledged constellation at all,[5] and Homer did not bother with whether it dipped or not. Or, alternatively, 700 B.C. must be abandoned as our date for Homer, and we must move the center of our horizon circles of latitude far back enough in time along the circle of polar precession to produce a horizon circle which will allow the Little Dipper to dip, but not the Big.

If we choose the first alternative and suppose that the Little Dipper was not a constellation for Homer in 700 B.C., then Homer could not, as has most often been supposed, have composed his poems in Chios at a latitude of 38½ degrees, his self-named heirs the Homeridae notwithstanding, nor at nearby Smyrna, or Kolophon. For our horizon circle of latitude clearly shows that at Chios in 700 B.C. the Dragon, one of the great Constellations, partook no more in the bath of ocean than did the Bear.

Moving south from Chios, our horizon circle of latitude shows that Pylos and Halicarnassos are both on latitude 37 degrees,[6] where Etamin, in Draco, barely skims the horizon. This is reason enough for me to exclude both cities, for to justify Homer's statement, all constellations, with the single exception of the Great Bear, must clearly dip below the horizon, and not just skim it. Halicarnassos does not figure at all in *The Odyssey*, so I am not particularly sorry to exclude her. Pylos, on the other hand, is tempting because of the poet's evident fondness for the place, and his admiration for its wise King Nestor. But historians and archaeologists have shown that after 1000 B.C. sandy Pylos was in ruins and firmly in the grip of the Dorians, which leaves the linguists to affirm that the Homeric epics are not likely to have been composed there, since there is no trace of Doric in Homer's language, which seems not to

5. Pannekoek, p. 95 (see Bibliography), says of this period: "The Little Bear was evidently not yet known."
6. See front endpaper. Note that the whole eastern Mediterranean, a Cypriot's home sea, lies below latitude 37 degrees.

have been an everyday language at all, but rather a poetic language related principally to Ionic and Aeolic. And the same linguistic argument that eliminates Pylos also excludes Crete and the rest of the important Greek world below a latitude of 37 degrees with one exception, Cyprus, which my chart shows to be so situated relative to the stars of 700 B.C. that faithfully every night even the Dragon took his bath, while the Great Bear remained vigilant and dry, silently circling the pole in pursuit of Orion, exactly as described in *The Odyssey*.

Having reached this navigational conclusion, I checked the possibility of a Cypriot Homer with my linguist friends, and was happy to find that they did not consider it impossible. Not only did the Cypriots in classical times continue to speak Arcadio-Cypriot, a language very similar to that of the Mycenaeans themselves and containing something of Ionic and much of Aeolic as well as some Oriental touches;[7] but, as has been shown in Chapter I, even when the rest of the Greek world had adopted the alphabet of Cyprus's neighbors the Phoenicians, the conservative islanders continued to write in a syllabic script not unlike that of the tablets from Pylos, whence their forebears were supposed to have migrated. Which opens up the intriguing possibility that a Cypriot Homer might have had access to actual Mycenaean records, and conserves the possibility of his connection with Nestor's Pylos, however indirect. The origin of *The Iliad*'s famous Catalogue of Ships would be neatly explained if a Cypriot Homer could have read the catalogue in the Pylian tablets, whose typical contents, as we have seen, were precisely such lists.[8] Also explained would be Homer's impartiality between Greeks and Trojans, which so closely reflects the neutrality of Cyprus in the Trojan War, for Homer says that the king of Cyprus conserved his alliance with Agamemnon with a gift, but sent no forces against his other allies the Trojans. All of which reminds us of the survival at Paphos of

7. Germain (see Bibliography).
8. Page is convinced that the catalogue must go back to an authentic Mycenaean source (see Bibliography).

the Goddess of the Pylian tablets, and also of the bard's own obvious predilection for the land of Navsikaa, which our search has already placed on Cyprus.

There remains the second alternative to the problem of the Little Dipper, which is to consider it as a constellation that must "dip," and the result is an amusing one: if we reduce the Great Bear to its absolute minimum, that is to the basic seven stars that give us the shape of the Chariot or Dipper (the Romans' Septentrion, the easiest shape to recognize with the naked eye), and if we run one point of our compass along the circle of precession while keeping the other on the Little Dipper's handle, Polaris, we find that when we reach the radius corresponding to a latitude of 30 degrees on our compass, the Little Dipper begins to dip its handle in the watery horizon, while the Big Dipper remains dry as prescribed, and all this approximately in the fourth millennium B.C.

Now, 30 degrees is the latitude of our city of the Phileni, or Lotuseaters, the southernmost point in the whole of the Mediterranean. So, strictly from the point of view of the stars, it is possible that Homer could have been a Lotus-eater who lived in the thirty-sixth century B.C., an intriguing possibility in this age of "mind-expanding" drugs. And carrying this process even further, it might even be held that Homer wrote in Chios after all, but in the sixth millennium B.C. You can also play at this game, reader, if you have a compass, and do not be discouraged by the fact that today you will find little company in the supposition that Troy fell many centuries before 1200 B.C. Even Ventris had only one ally when he proposed his deciphering of the tablets. As for me, I am satisfied with Cyprus for Homer and 1200 B.C. for the fall of Troy.

I took off on my last Odyssean flight to check my "Cypriot Homer" with V. Karageorghis, Director of Antiquities of Cyprus, to whom Marinatos had kindly given me an introduction. He received me most cordially, and far from deriding my theory, forthwith invited me to a locked room in the museum's basement, where he showed me his latest finds, not yet published. There were several pieces, all apparently My-cenaean, the most impressive a beautiful chair of wood inlaid with ivory in spiral designs that I immediately recognized not only from *The Odyssey* but also from the tablets. And the extraordinary thing is that these "Mycenaean" objects have been dated by Karageorghis as having been in use in Cyprus in the seventh or eighth century B.C., one more example of the Cypriots' secular conservatism. Thus our Cypriot Homer could not only have read tablets possibly inherited from his Pylian an-cestors; he could also have been familiar with furniture and artifacts of the thirteenth-century world he wrote about. And since the seventh and eighth centuries saw the greatest development of astronomy in the Middle East, Cypriot Homer's knowledgeable use of the stars should not surprise us; a man who so describes the sea and the heavens below latitude 37 degrees must often have sailed the eastern Mediterranean under the stars. I later met Karageorghis again in New York, and he told me of new finds of "Mycenaean" artifacts of the eighth century B.C., agreed with my emphasis on the similarities between the Cretan and Cypriot alphabets, and gave me the photograph of "Penelope's Chair," which I gratefully reproduce.[9]

One more journey encouraged me to present my Cypriot Homer, this one to New York, where I visited the Hayden Planetarium, direct de-scendant of the one whose remains have been found in a third-century wreck near Antikithara, close to where Ulysses was blown away from Malea. At the Hayden I checked with a technician, Mr. Quinn, who assured me that my star theories could be cranked into the planetarium's "time machine," as long as they were concerned only with stars and not with wayward planets. So I went to Mr. Kenneth L. Franklin, assistant director of the planetarium and in charge during the director's absence, and he was immediately so interested that we spent the rest of the after-noon checking astronomical tables. As soon as the public "show" was over he turned the planetarium over to me, and we moved the artificial

9. See photo page 171.

"Penelope's Chair"

heavens back to the dates and latitudes that interested me. My two eldest sons were with me, and they watched in awe from the center of the great empty vault as the artificial skies confirmed my conclusions as to the behavior of the stars at those latitudes and dates which concern us. I, in turn, was happy to prove to them that one can still reach relatively precise and complex conclusions with a school compass, conclusions that one can later check with the marvelous equipment that today serves us so well as long as it does not become indispensable.

So we come to the end of our airborne Odyssey with the comforting thought that history can be tracked down by means as modern as an aircraft or as primitive as a draftsman's compass, and also from the point of view of a single discipline such as navigation, or of many, such as archaeology, linguistics, astronomy, and finally even astronautics.[10]

Still on the Greek wind, our own northeaster, Lita and I flew home to the high *Sabana* of Bogotá, which, Andean as it is, now had for us an air of Arcady; for Greece is everywhere for those who love her. And I trust, reader, that during our search, we have relived together the Greeks' greatest poem, full of sorrow and of joy, and therefore of beauty. For as our Muses disappear again beyond the wine-dark sea, it seems to me that they leave us this thought: Man will be able to add beauty to this world so long as he can bring a smile, or even a tear, to the many faces of his God, and it is perhaps for this that he was created.

10. See photo page 173.

God's-Eye View of the Mediterranean, from NASA Satellite

QUOTATIONS FROM THE ODYSSEY

ULYSSES' SCHEDULE

SHORT BIBLIOGRAPHY

INDEX

QUOTATIONS FROM THE ODYSSEY

The minor Roman numerals refer to my text, and the corresponding passages from *The Odyssey* are identified by major Roman numerals for chapters or books, and by Arabic numbers for lines. Because of my paraphrasing of Homer's text, some elasticity will be necessary in locating certain quotations, depending also on the Homeric text used by the reader.

CHAPTER I *(pages 13–48)*

i. *Book* IV. 172.
ii. II. 148.
iii. IV. 649.
iv. VI. 187.
v. II. 181.
vi. III. 430.
vii. III. 154.

viii. III. 157.
ix. III. 276.
x. II. 424.
xi. II. 88, 118.
xii. I. 433.
xiii. III. 272.
xiv. I. 214.

xv. IV. 737.
xvi. IV. 818.
xvii. IV. 71.
xviii. II. 337.
xix. III. 465.
xx. IV. 127.

CHAPTER II *(pages 51–90)*

i. *Book* IX. 39.
ii. IX. 39, IX. 67.

iii. IX. 100.
iv. IX. 181.

v. IX. 528.
vi. X. 1.

CHAPTER III *(pages 93–129)*

i. *Book* X. 55.
ii. X. 125.
iii. X. 194.
iv. XI. 74.
v. X. 277.
vi. X. 489.
vii. X. 190.

viii. XI. 13.
ix. X. 505.
x. XI. 57.
xi. XI. 128.
xii. XI. 134.
xiii. XI. 488.

xiv. XII. 3.
xv. XII. 39.
xvi. XII. 184.
xvii. XII. 55.
xviii. XII. 127.
xix. XII. 403.

CHAPTER IV (pages 133–160)

CHAPTER V (pages 163–173)

ULYSSES' SCHEDULE

Leave Troy	Early fall
Land of the Lotus-eaters, and	Fall
Land of the Laistrygones	
Land of the Cyclopes	Late fall
With Circe (Aiaia)	One year
Hades	Late fall (second year)
Skylla and Charybdis	Late spring (third year)
With Kalypso (Ogygia)	Seven years
With Navsikaa	Late summer
Return to Ithaka	Fall (tenth year)

SHORT BIBLIOGRAPHY

A Homeric bibliography can be endless, so here are a few of the works that seem pertinent to *Ulysses Airborne,* though most of them disagree with some of my identifications.

Bagrow, Leo. *History of Cartography.* Edited by R. A. Skelton, Cambridge, Mass.: Harvard University Press, 1964.

Bass, George F. *Archaeology under Water.* London: Thames and Hudson, 1966.

Berard, Victor. *Les Navigations d'Ulysse.* Paris: Librairie Armand Colin, 1935.

————. *Dans le sillage d'Ulysse. Album Odysséen* (out of print).

Blegen, Carl W., with M. Rawson. *The Palace of Nestor at Pylos in Western Messenia.* Princeton, N.J.: Princeton University Press, 1966.

Bourdeaux, P. M. *Pour le Yachting—Routes de la Mediterranée.* Eds. Maritimes et d'Outre-Mer, 1966.

Bradford, Ernle. *Ulysses Found.* New York: Harcourt, Brace & World, 1963.

Buchner, Giorgio. "Pithekoussai, Oldest Greek Colony in the West." *Expedition,* vol. 8, No. 4 (Summer 1966).

Carpenter, Rhys. *Folk-Tale, Fiction, and Saga in the Homeric Epics.* Berkeley: University of California Press, 1949.

Cartilhac, Emile. *Monuments Primitifs aux Iles Baléares.* Toulouse, France: Lib. Edouard Privat, 1892.

Casson, Lionel, "The Sails of the Ancient Mariner," *Archaeology,* vol. 7, No. 4, 1954.

Chadwick, John. *Decypherment of Linear B.* Cambridge: Cambridge University Press, 1967.

Cottrell, Leonard. *The Lion Gate*. London: Evans Bros., 1964.

Davies, N. de G. *The Rock Tombs of Deir el Gebrâwi*, Part II, Plate XIX. Egypt Exploration Fund, London and Boston: 1902.

Dufour, Méderic. *L'Odyssée*. Translated by Jeanne Raison. Paris: Eds. Garnier Frères, 1961.

Dumas, Frédéric. *Epaves Antiques*. Paris: Maisonneuve de Larose, 1968.

Du Plat Taylor, Joan. *Marine Archaeology*, London: Hutchinson, 1965.

Finley, M. I. *The World of Odysseus*. New York: Viking Press, 1954.

Germain, Gabriel. *Genèse de l'Odyssée*. Presses Universitaires de France, 1954.

Herodotos. *Famous History*. London: Constable and Co., Ltd. 1924.

Hesiod. *The Works and Days*. Ann Arbor: University of Michigan Press, 1968.

Heuvelmans, Bernard. *In the Wake of the Sea Serpents*. New York: Hill and Wang, 1968.

Honoré, Pierre. *La Leyenda de los Dioses Blancos*. Barcelona: Ed. Destino, 1965.

Hope Simpson, R. *A Gazetteer and Atlas of Mycenaean Sites*. London: Institute of Classical Studies, University of London, 1965.

Kiepert, Heinrich. *Atlas Antiquus*. Berlin: Dietrich Reimer, N.D.

Kirchenbauer, Anton. *Beiträge zur Homerischen Uranologie*. Wien: 1874.

Kirk, G. S. *Ships on Geometric Vases*. London: Annual of the British School at Athens, 44 (1949).

Lattimore, Richmond (translator). *The Odyssey of Homer*. Harper & Row, 1967.

Lorimer, H. L. *Stars and Constellations in Homer and Hesiod*. London: Annual of the British School at Athens, 1951.

Marinatos, Spyridon. "La Marine Creto-Mycenienne." *Bulletin de Correspondance Hellenique*, 57 (1933).

———. "Minoan and Cretan Civilization and Its Influence on the Mediterranean and Northern Europe." VI International Congress on Prehistoric and Protohistoric Science, Rome, 1968.

Marinatos, Spyridon, and Hilmer, Max. *Crete and Mycenae.* London: Thames and Hudson, 1960.

Morison, Samuel E. *Spring Tides.* Boston: Houghton Mifflin Co., 1965.

Moulinier, Louis. *Geographie d'Homère dans l'Odyssée.* Aix-en-Provence: *Editions Ophrys,* 1958.

Mylonas, Carl. "Priam's Troy and the Date of Its Fall." *Hesperia,* 33 (1964).

Neugebauer, O. "Ancient Mathematics and Astronomy." A *History of Technology.* Edited by C. J. Singer *et al.* Oxford: Oxford University Press, 1954.

Nordenskiöld, Adolf E. *Periplus, The Early History of Charts and Sailing Directions.* New York: Burt Franklin (originally Stockholm, 1897).

Page, Denys. *History and the Homeric Iliad.* Berkeley: University of California Press, 1959.

Palmer, Leonard R. *Mycenaeans and Minoans.* London: Faber and Faber Ltd., 1965.

Pannekoek, A. A *History of Astronomy.* London: G. Allen and Unwin, 1961.

Pillot, Gilbert. *Le Code Secret de l'Odyssée.* Paris: Robert Laffont, 1969.

Ptolomaeus, Claudius. *Cosmographia.* Bologna 1477. Ulm 1482. *Theatrum Orbis Terrarum.* Amsterdam: Meridian Co., 1963.

Quintus of Smyrna. *The War at Troy, What Homer Didn't Tell.* Norman: University of Oklahoma Press, 1968.

Renault, Mary. *The Bull from the Sea.* London: The New English Library, 1968.

Rieu, E. V. (translator). *The Odyssey.* Baltimore: Penguin Books, 1951.

Sandys, Sir John. *A History of Classical Scholarship*. Cambridge, England: Cambridge University Press, 1921.

Scrra, María Luisa. "Menorca, Piedra y Arqueología," in *Menorca, la Isla desconocida*. Barcelona: Ed. Barna, 1964.

Slocum, Joshua. *Sailing Alone Around the World*. New York: Grosset & Dunlap, 1954.

United States Oceanographic Office (U.S.H.O.): *Sailing Directions for the Mediterranean*, 1958, rev. 1968.

Vermeule, Emily. *Greece in the Bronze Age*. Chicago: University of Chicago Press, 1964.

Wace, A. J. B., and Stubbings, F. H. *A Companion to Homer*. London: Macmillan Company, 1962.

INDEX

Maa, Cyprus, 144
Magellan, Ferdinand, 4
Mago, 64, 77
Mahón, 76, 77, 84
Málaga, 89, 110
Malea, Cape, 30, 31, 58, 60–63, 66, 159, 170
Mallorca, 70–81, 84; caves, 76–77, 81
Malta, 133–136
Marfak (star), 101n.
Marinatos, Spyridion, 7, 62–63, 149, 169
Maron, 45n., 53–54
Maronia, 53
Marrakesh, 97
Martí, Francisco, 7, 77
Mediterranean Sea, satellite view, 173
Meganisi, 154–155, 158
Meges, 155, 158
Meltemi, 38, 54–57, 63, 66
Menelaos, 2, 22, 23, 29–31, 41–42, 57, 58, 152, 156, 158; Telemachos at court of, 42–43, 45, 48
Mentor, 31, 41
Messina, 64, 128
Messina, Strait of, 117, 121, 124, 128, 135
Mestro, 40
Mijas, 110
Minix, *see* Djerba
Minorca, 64, 76–82, 84, 94, 99, 151; archaeology, 76–77; cave dwelling, 82; coast of bronze, 84, 88; Isla del Aire, 84, 86, 87; *navetas*, 76, 79, 85; Polyphemos' cave, 78, 79; *taulas*, 76, 79, 80
Morison, Patricia, 3, 6
Morison, Samuel Eliot, 3–4, 6, 7, 63
Mycenaeans (Achaeans or Argives), 21; chair, "Penelope's," 170, 171; exports and imports, 46; religion, 21–28; ship, 32, 137, 139, 141; wine, 45–46, 48; writing, 13–18
Mykene, 14–16; tablets, 15; Tholos tombs, 25, 26

Najar, Victor, 7, 32n.
Naples, 108

Nauplia (Argos), 57–58
Navetas, 76, 79, 85
Navigation: latitude sailing, 100–101, 103; stars in, 101, 102, 138, 164–165
Navsikaa, 1, 24, 117, 139, 140, 142–151, 169
Neleus, 16, 43
Nestor, 2, 16, 22, 32, 46, 54, 58, 107, 114, 167; palace of, 43, 44, 47; sacrifice, 27–28; ships and voyage, 30–31, 52–53; Telemachos visits, 43, 48, 147
Nicosia, 142
Nidri, 158
Nields, James F., 4, 7
Noëmon, 24, 157–158
Nordenskiöld, Adolf E., 68n.
Norsemen, 4, 34
Numbers, magical, 40

Obregón, Lita (Cristina), 4, 6, 13, 18–20, 60, 63, 64, 66, 69, 75, 79, 81, 84, 89, 97, 99, 103, 110–111, 116, 117, 121, 135, 141, 149, 152, 172
Obregón, Rafael, 3, 7, 150
Ocean, ancient concept of, 36, 38, 110, 114
Odyssey, 36, 40, 84, 101, 156, 163; end of, 159–160; gods in, 22–24; luxury in, 42–44; ships in, 30–32, 34; structure of, 1–3; women in, 41–42
Ogygia, 2, 84, 128, 133–135
Oh Papa, airplane, 3–6, 18–20, 32, 48, 58, 68, 75, 81, 97, 108, 116, 128, 133, 149, 152, 160
Olympos, 36
Opel, Fritz von, 7
Orestes, 41
Orion (constellation), 40, 138, 164
Orpheus, 151

Palermo, 129
Palmer, Leonard R., 28
Papanastasiou, pilot, 62
Paper, 18n.
Paphos, 141, 142, 144, 145, 147, 148, 168–169
Paris (person), 40, 41

About the Author

MAURICIO OBREGÓN, Colombian born in 1921, was educated at Stonyhurst, Oxford, M.I.T., and Harvard. He speaks six languages and holds a degree in engineering and a diploma in architecture.

An officer of the Colombian Air Force and of the British Army, during the Second World War he flew as engineering test captain at Grumman Aircraft on Long Island. Then he founded an airline in Colombia for which he built half a dozen airports; edited *Semana* newsmagazine; and organized the Aeronautics Department and the Interoceanic Canal Corporation for the Colombian government. Elected president of the International Aviation Federation, he established an Olympic world lightplane speed record.

Having helped to found the University of the Andes in Bogotá, he served as Trustee and Vice-Rector, as well as Chairman of the Colombian Educational Radio Network, the largest in the Americas. He has also been Colombian Ambassador to Venezuela and to the O.A.S. in Washington.

His wife, Cristina Martínez-Irujo, was born in Madrid. Doubling as photographer, she has accompanied her husband in his plane all over North and South America as well as Eastern and Western Europe, mostly in pursuit of the history of discovery. They have six children and make their home, if anywhere, in Bogotá.

Mr. Obregón is co-author, with Samuel Eliot Morison, of *The Caribbean as Columbus Saw It*.

71 72 73 10 9 8 7 6 5 4 3 2 1

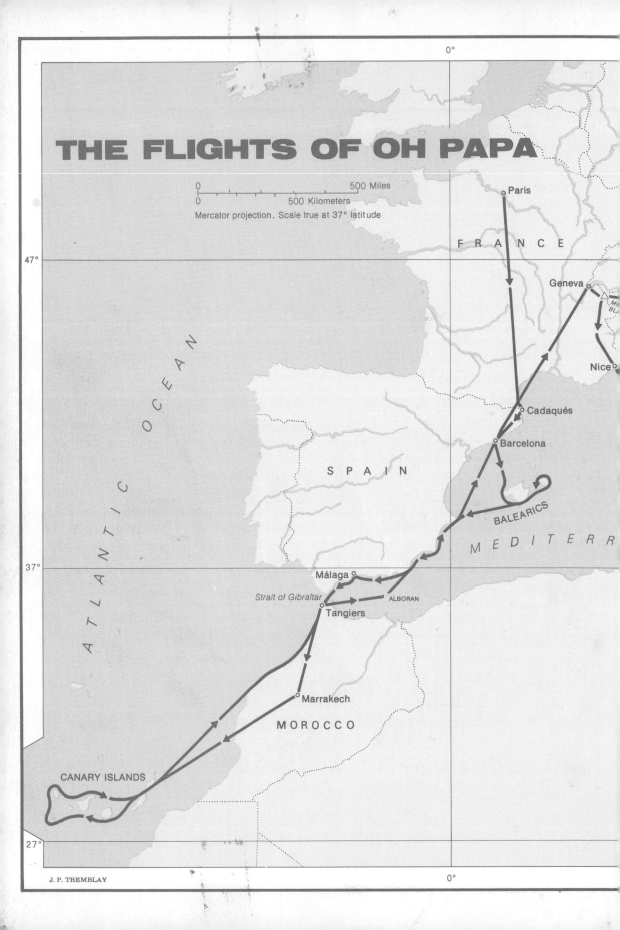